BILLIARDS

THE OFFICIAL RULES & RECORDS BOOK

1991

**BILLIARD CONGRESS
OF AMERICA**

BCA RULES COMMITTEE

Chairman: Jerry Briesath; Gary Benson, Randy Goettlicher,
Peg Ledman, Richard Rhorer

BCA STATISTICS/RECORDS COMMITTEE

Chairman: Michael Shamos; Bruce Venske, Gary Benson

Published By
BILLIARD CONGRESS OF AMERICA
1901 Broadway St., Suite 310
Iowa City, Iowa 52240
(319)351-2112

ISBN 1-878493-01-9
ISSN 1047-244

FOREWORD

The Billiard Congress of America came into existence in 1947 along with the now defunct National Billiard Council. From its beginning, BCA has attempted to unify our industry; bringing together player, proprietor, retailer and manufacturer. The rules contained in this book were established with this goal in mind, hoping to facilitate a better understanding of billiards.

We wish to recognize the Rules Committee, noted on the previous page, for their dedication and contribution to this effort.

Mission Statement of the Billiard Congress of America

The mission of the BCA is to govern and promote the sport of billiards (pocket, three-cushion and snooker) in the United States and world-wide by establishing rules and equipment specifications, promoting and sanctioning amateur and professional tournaments and helping to increase awareness of and participation in the sport to all people, while working with all integers to increase the overall growth of billiards. BCA will perform all of its functions on a non-profit basis with the highest ethical standards and fair treatment of all of its members and the entire billiards community.

TABLE OF CONTENTS

THE ANCIENT & HONORABLE GAME OF BILLIARDS

The first reference to billiard tables was made in the year 1400, according to author and billiard historian William Hendricks. Undoubtedly, the table version was derived from yard bowling, which is mentioned in records dating back to the 10th century. Most references were made in connection with games played by royalty in the countries of France, Spain, Holland and Scotland. By the 16th century, billiards had earned a less elegant reputation as a diversion for scoundrels in the taverns of England – thereby instigating a bone of contention that has been gnawed upon for 400 years.

Unlike the modern product, the pocketless table had arches or wickets, and the balls of wood (later ivory) were pushed with the blunt end of a crooked stick called a mace. The cue, as we know it today, did not come into being until the early 1800's, when an imprisoned French officer named Mingaud discovered that a leather tipped cue resulted in much greater control over a struck ball. Thus was invented "english".

Billiards came to America with the Spanish in 1565. It spread westward with the French and Spanish expansion of the country, and was duly noted upon its arrival in such frontier villages as New Orleans and St. Louis. Likewise, the British brought their version, Snooker, to the New England, as they did to all of the other colonies of their growing empire.

Billiards, the intriguing, ever-evolving sport, grew steadily in popularity in the United States through the 1800's and early 1900's, reaching its zenith in the 1920's.

Today, the game has continued its metamorphosis and is enjoying a resurgence. The legendary billiard rooms of yesteryear now share their customers with the corner tavern, the college campus and the family recreation room. Straight pool shares the limelight with Eight-Ball and Nine-Ball. And the enthusiasm of the players is as great as ever. Thirty-six million strong – young and old, men and women – they eagerly await the challenge that is certain to come wherever a table is found. Good playing to you.

BCA EQUIPMENT SPECIFICATIONS

TABLE SIZES:

Pocket Pool Tables .... 4 by 8 and 4 ^{1}/$_2$ by 9
Carom Billiard Tables .... 4 ^{1}/$_2$ by 9 and 5 by 10
American Snooker Tables .... 4 ^{1}/$_2$ by 9 and 5 by 10

PLAYING AREA:

Measured from the cloth covered nose of cushion rubber, to the opposite cushion rubber, both width and length:

4 by 8 table .... playing area of 46" width by 92" length
4 ^{1}/$_2$ by 9 table .... playing area of 50" width by 100" length
5 by 10 table .... playing area of 56" width by 112" length

BCA will sanction Tournament Play on Home and Coin-operated tables, produced in sizes other than those recognized above, if the playing area width is one-half the length, measured cushion to opposite cushion.

TABLE BED HEIGHT:

The table bed playing surface, when measured from the bottom of the table leg, will be 29 ^{1}/$_4$" (plus or minus ^{1}/$_4$").

POCKET OPENINGS:

Pocket pool tables: pocket openings are measured between opposing cushion noses at the points where the nose changes direction into the pocket throat.

Corner .... 4 ^{7}/$_8$" minimum to 5 ^{1}/$_8$" maximum
Side .... 5 ^{3}/$_8$" minimum to 5 ^{5}/$_8$" maximum

Snooker tables: pocket openings are measured between the opposing cushion noses at the point where the nose meets the slate opening in the pocket throat.

Corner .... 3 ^{3}/$_8$" minimum to 3 ^{5}/$_8$" maximum
Side .... 4 ^{1}/$_{16}$" maximum

PLAYING BED:

The playing surface must be capable, either by its own strength or a combination of its strength and that of the table baseframe, of maintaining an overall flatness within ± .020" lengthwise and .010" across the width. Further, this surface should have an additional deflection not to exceed .030" when loaded with a concentrated static force of 200 pounds at its center. If more than one slab is employed, the slab joints must be in the same plane within .005" after leveling and shiming. This surface must be capable of withstanding without fracture or indentation the impact of a 6 ounce billiard ball dropped 6' above the surface. The bed must be covered with a billiard fabric, the major portion of which is made of wool, with

2

proper tension to avoid unwanted ball roll-off (one ball diameter maximum). Weight must be a minimum of 130 lb. per cubic foot. Commercial table must have a 1"-3 piece set of slate with a wooden frame minimum $^3/_4$" attached to slate. All playing surfaces must be secured to base frame with screws or bolts.

CUSHION:

Rubber cushions should be triangular in shape and molded with the conventional K-66 profile with a base of 1 $^3/_{16}$" and a nose height of 1", with control fabric molded to the top and base area of the cushion. On carom and snooker tables, the triangular K-66 profile cushion is to be maintained, however, the control fabric may be modified to affect a medium or slow speed ball rebound action. The balance of the rail section to which the rubber cushion is glued should be of hard-wood construction and attached to the slate bed with a minimum of three (3) heavy duty, threaded rail bolts per rail.

BILLIARD BALLS:

Molded and finished in a perfect sphere, with both dynamic and static balance, in the following weights and diameters as used in the following games:

Pocket Pool Balls

   Weight: 5 $^1/_2$ to 6 oz. .... *Diameter: 2 $^1/_4$"

Carom Balls

   Weight: 7 to 7 $^1/_2$ oz. .... *Diameter: 2 $^{27}/_{64}$"

                                                                               2 $^3/_8$"

                                                                                2 $^7/_{16}$"

Snooker Balls

   Weight: 5 to 5 $^1/_2$ oz. .... *Diameter 2 $^1/_8$"

                                                                              2 $^1/_{16}$"

*Diameter tolerance of (plus or minus) .005

Diagram No. 1

GLOSSARY OF BILLIARD TERMS

The following glossary contains those billiard terms and definitions essential to utilization of the rules of games provided in this book. In addition to definitions of such terms, there are also many references to equipment, accessories and phrases in common usage by billiard players.

Each definition begins with the term in bold face type, followed by a parenthetical notation of the game variation or classification in which the term is used, or to which it primarily applies.

Where a diagram or other supplemental information is available elsewhere in this book, it is referenced parenthetically following the definition.

ANGLED. (Snooker, pocket games) When the corner of a pocket prevents a player shooting the cue ball directly at an object ball. (Also see *corner-hooked*.)

ANGLE SHOT. (Pocket games) A shot that requires the cue ball to drive the object ball other than straight ahead. (Also see *cut shot*.)

APEX OF TRIANGLE. (Pocket games) The position in the grouping of object balls that is on the *foot spot*; the front ball position of the *pyramid* or *rack*.

AROUND THE TABLE. (Carom games) Describes shots in which the cue ball contacts three or more cushions, usually including the two short cushions, in an effort to score.

BALANCE POINT. (General) The point on a cue at which it would remain level if held by a single support; usually about 18" from the butt end of the cue.

BALL IN HAND. (Pocket games) See *cue ball in hand*.

BALL ON. (Snooker) A colored (non-red) ball a player intends to legally pocket; same as *on ball*.

BANK SHOT. (Pocket games) A shot on which the object ball is driven to one or more cushions before it is pocketed; incidental contact as a ball moves along and adjacent to a cushion does not qualify as a cushion or bank. It is not an obvious shot and must be called in games requiring called shots. (also see *kick shot*.)

BED OF TABLE. (General) The flat, cloth-covered surface of the table within the cushions; the playing area exclusive of the cushions.

BILLIARD. (Carom games) A count or score; a successful shot.

BLIND DRAW. (General) A method used to determine pairings or bracketing of players in tournaments that assures totally random placement or pairing of contestants.

BOTTLE. (Pocket games) A specially shaped leather or plastic container used in various games; also called the *shake bottle*.

BREAK. (Pocket games) See *open break* and *opening break shot*.

BREAK. (Snooker) Total scored in one inning.

BREAKING VIOLATION. (Pocket games) A violation of special rules which apply only to the *opening break* shot of certain games. Unless specified in individual game rules, a breaking violation is not a foul.

BRIDGE. (General) The hand configuration that holds and guides the shaft-end of the cue during play; also see *mechanical bridge*.

BURST. (Forty-One Pocket Billiards) Scoring a total of more than 41 points.

BUTT OF CUE. (General) The larger end of a cue, opposite the tip. On a two-piece cue, the butt extends up to the joint.

CALL SHOT. (Pocket games) Requirement that a player designate, in advance of each shot, the ball to be made and the pocket into which it will be made.

CALLED BALL. (Pocket games) The ball the player has designated to be pocketed on a shot effort.

CALLED POCKET. (Pocket games) The pocket into which a player has designated a ball to be made.

CAROM. (General) To bounce off or glance off an object ball or cushion; a shot in which the cue ball bounces off one ball into another is termed a carom.

CAROM, SCORING. (General) Contact by the cue ball with object balls, the bottle or cushions in such a way that a legal score is made, according to specific game rules.

CENTER SPOT. (General) The exact center point of a table's playing surface.

CHALK. (General) A dry, slightly abrasive substance that is applied to the cue tip to help assure a non-slip contact between the cue tip and the cue ball.

CHUCK NURSE. (Straight Rail Billiards) A scoring technique used when one object ball rests against the cushion and the second object ball is to one side of the first ball and away from the cushion. Cue ball strikes the object ball at the cushion so that the cue ball just comes back to touch (carom) the second object ball without moving it out of position for a similar subsequent shot.

CLEAN BANK. (Bank Pocket Billiards) A shot in which the object ball being played does not touch any other object balls (i.e., no kisses, no combinations).

CLEAR BALL. (Carom games) The all-white ball, devoid of any markings, used in carom games. (Also see *spot ball*.)

COMBINATION. (Pocket games) Shot in which the cue ball first strikes a ball other than the one to be pocketed, with the ball initially contacted in turn striking one or more other balls in an effort to score.

COMBINATION ON. (Pocket games) Two or more balls positioned in such a way that a ball can be driven into a called pocket with a combination shot; often called a "dead combo" or an "on combo."

COMBINATION ON. (Snooker) See *plant*.

CONTACT POINT. (General) The precise point of contact between the cue ball and the object ball when the cue ball strikes the object ball. *(*See **Instructional Playing Tips.***)*

CORNER HOOKED. (Pocket games, Snooker) When the corner of a pocket prevents shooting the cue ball in a straight path directly to an object ball, the cue ball is corner hooked; same as angled.

COUNT. (General) A score; a successful shot.

COUNT, THE. (General) The running score at any point during a player's inning in games where numerous points are scored successively.

CROSS CORNER. (Pocket games) Term used to describe a *bank shot* that will rebound from a cushion and into a corner pocket.

CROSS SIDE. (Pocket games) Term used to describe a *bank shot* that will rebound from a cushion into a side pocket.

CROSS TABLE SHOT. (Carom games) Shot in which scoring is accomplished by driving the cue ball across the table between the long cushions.

CROTCH. (Carom games) The corner area of a carom table. The four crotches are defined as those spaces within crotch lines drawn between points on the side and end cushions 4 1/2 inches from the corners of the playing surface to the cushions.

CRUTCH. (General) Slang term for the *mechanical bridge*.

CUE. (General) Tapered device, usually wooden, used to strike the cue ball to execute carom or pocket billiard shots. Also called "cue stick."

CUE BALL. (General) The white, unnumbered ball that is always struck by the cue during play.

CUE BALL IN HAND. (Pocket games) Cue ball may be put into play anywhere on the playing surface.

CUE BALL IN HAND BEHIND THE HEAD STRING. (Pocket games) Cue ball may be put into play anywhere between the head string and the cushion on the head end of the table not in contact with an object ball. (See Diagram #1, Pg. 4.)

CUE TIP. (General) A piece of specially processed leather attached to the shaft end of the cue that contacts the cue ball when a shot is executed.

CUSHION. (General) The cloth covered rubber which borders the inside of the rails on carom and pocket billiard tables; together the cushions form the outer perimeter of the basic playing surface.

CUT SHOT. (Pocket games) A shot in which the cue ball contacts the object ball to one side or the other of full center, thus driving it in a direction other than that of the initial cue ball path. (See **Instructional Playing Tips.**)

"D." (Snooker) An area, semi-circular in shape, with the straight side formed by the head string and the semi-circle being prescribed by an arc drawn with the head spot as the center point. The radius of the semi-circle is determined by the size of the table being used. (See Diagram #11, Pg. 95.)

DEAD BALL. (Pocket games) A cue ball stroked in such a manner that virtually all of the speed and/or spin of the cue ball is transferred to the object ball, the cue ball retaining very little or none after contact.

DEAD BALL SHOT. (Pocket games) A shot in which a "dead ball" stroke is employed; often called a "kill" shot, because of the relative lack of cue ball motion after contact with the object ball.

DEAD COMBINATION. (Pocket games) See *combination on.*

DIAMONDS. (General) Inlays or markings on the table rails that are used as reference or target points. Though used in pocket games, the diamonds are essential for the utilization of numerous mathematical systems employed by carom games players. (See **The Diamond System.**)

DRAW SHOT. (General) A shot in which the cue ball is struck below center with an effective stroke, resulting in the cue ball reversing direction after contact with the object ball, because of the underspin applied to the cue ball.

DROP POCKETS. (Pocket games) Type of pockets with no automatic return of the balls to the foot end of the table; balls must be removed manually.

DOUBLE DRAW SHOT. (General) A shot in which such extreme and effective draw stroke is employed that when the cue ball reverses direction after contact with the object ball into a cushion and rebounds, the underspin (draw) overcomes the direction and speed of the rebound, causing the cue ball to stop and reverse direction again.

DOUBLE ELIMINATION. (General) A tournament format in which a player is not eliminated until he has sustained two match losses.

DOUBLE HIT. (General) A shot on which the cue ball is struck twice by the cue tip on the same stroke. (Also refer to General Rules of Pocket Billiards, Carom Billiards.)

DOUBLE ROUND ROBIN. (General) A tournament format in which each contestant in a field plays each of the other players twice.

ENGLISH. (General) Side spin applied to the cue ball by striking it off center; used to alter the natural roll of the cue ball and/or the object ball.

FEATHER SHOT. (General) A shot in which the cue ball barely touches or grazes the object ball; an extremely thin cut.

FERRULE. (General) A piece of protective material (usually white ivory or plastic) at the end of the cue shaft, onto which the cue tip is attached.

FOLLOW SHOT. (General) A shot in which the cue ball is struck above center, resulting in the cue ball continuing in the same general direction of the stroke with the object ball. Because of the overspin applied to the cue ball, the speed of the cue ball will be faster than that of natural roll.

FOLLOW-THROUGH. (General) The movement of the cue after contact with the cue ball through the area previously occupied by the cue ball. (See **Instructional Playing Tips.**)

FOOT OF TABLE. (General) The end of a carom or pocket billiard table at which the balls are racked or positioned at the start of a game.

FOOT SPOT. (General) The point on the foot end of the table where imaginary lines drawn between the center diamonds of the short rails and the second diamonds of the long rails intersect. (See Diagram #1, Pg. 4.)

FOOT STRING. (General) A line on the foot end of the table between the second diamonds of the long rails, passing through the foot spot. (See Diagram #1, Pg. 4.)

FORCE. (General) The inertia or power applied on the stroke to the cue ball, which may result in distortion and altering of natural angles and action of the ball.

FORCE DRAW. (General) Extreme underspin applied to the cue ball; usually refers to shots in which the cue ball first travels in the direction of the stroke for a distance before the underspin takes effect and the cue balls tops and then draws back in a generally opposite direction.

FORCE FOLLOW. (General) An extreme follow shot, with the term generally used in reference to shots in which the cue ball is shot directly at and then "through" an object ball, with a pronounced hesitation or stop before the overspin propels the cue ball forward in the general direction of the stroke.

FOUL. (General) An infraction of the rules of play, as defined in either the general or the specific game rules. (Not all rule infractions are fouls.) Fouls result in a penalty, also dependent on specific game rules.

FOUL STROKE. (General) A stroke on which a foul takes place.

FREE BREAK. (Pocket games) An opening break shot in which a wide spread of the object balls may be achieved without penalty or risk. Free breaks are detailed in individual games rules.

FROZEN. (General) A ball touching another ball or cushion.

FULL BALL. (General) Contact of the cue ball with an object ball at a contact point on a line bisecting the centers of the cue ball and object ball. (Also see **Instructional Playing Tips.**)

GAME BALL. (General) The ball which, if pocketed legally, would produce victory in a game.

GATHER SHOT. (Carom games) A shot on which appropriate technique and speed is employed to drive one or more balls away from the other(s) in such a manner that when the stroke is complete, the balls have come back together closely enough to present a comparatively easy scoring opportunity for the next shot.

GRIP. (General) The manner in which the butt of the cue is held in the hand. (Also see **Instructional Playing Tips.**)

GULLY TABLE. (Pocket games) A table with pockets and a return system that delivers the balls as they are pocketed to a collection bin on the foot end of the table.

HANDICAPPING. (General) Modifications in the scoring and/or rules of games to enable players of differing abilities to compete on more even terms.

HEAD OF TABLE. (General) The end of a carom or pocket billiard table from which the opening break is performed; the end normally marked with the manufacturer's nameplate.

HEAD SPOT. (General) The point on the head of the table where imaginary lines drawn between the center diamonds of the short rails and the second diamonds of the long rails intersect. (Diagram #1, Pg. 4.)

HEAD STRING. (General) A line on the head end of the table between the second diamonds of the long rails, passing through the head spot. (See Diagram #1, Pg. 4.)

HIGH RUN. (14.1 Continuous) During a specified segment of play, the greatest number of balls scored in one turn (inning) at the table.

HOLD. (General) *English* which stops the cue ball from continuing the course of natural roll it would take after having been driven in a certain direction.

INNING. (General) A turn at the table by a player.

IN HAND. (Pocket games) See *cue ball in hand.*

IN HAND BEHIND THE HEAD STRING. (Pocket games) See *cue ball in hand behind the head string.*

IN THE RACK. (Pocket games) A ball that would interfere with the re-racking of the object balls in games that extend past one rack.

JAW. (Pocket games) The slanted part of the cushion that is cut at an angle to form the opening from the bed of the table into the pocket.

JAWED BALL. (Pocket games) Generally refers to a ball that fails to drop because it bounces back and forth against the jaws of a pocket.

JOINT. (General) On two-piece cues, the screw-and-thread device, approximately midway in the cue, that permits it to be "broken down" into two separate sections.

JUMP SHOT. (General) A shot in which the cue ball and/or an object ball is caused to rise off the bed of the table.

JUMPED BALL. (General) A ball that has left and remained off of the playing surface as the result of a stroke.

KEY BALL. (14.1 Continuous) The 14th ball of each rack; called the key ball because it is so critical in obtaining position for the all important first (or break) shot of each rerack of the balls.

KICK SHOT. (General) a shot in which the cue ball banks off a cushion(s) prior to making contact with an object ball or scoring.

KILL SHOT. (Pocket games) See *dead ball shot.*

KISS. (General) Contact between balls. (Also see *kiss shot.*)

KISS SHOT. (Pocket games) A shot in which more than one contact with object balls is made by the cue ball; for example, the cue ball might kiss from one object ball into another to score the latter ball. Also shots in which object balls carom off one or more other object balls to be pocketed. (Also called *carom* shots.)

KISS-OUT. (General) Contact - accidental contact between balls that causes a shot to fail.

KITCHEN. (Pocket games) A slang term used to describe the area of the table between the head string and the cushion on the head end of the table. (Also called the area behind the head string.)

LAG. (Carom games) A shot in which the cue ball is shot three or more cushions before contacting the object balls.

LAG FOR BREAK. (General) Procedure used to determine starting player of game. Each player shoots a ball from behind the head string to the foot cushion, attempting to return the ball as closely as possible to the head cushion. (Also see **General Rules of Pocket Billiards, Carom Billiards.**)

LEAVE. (Pocket games) The position of the balls after a player's shot.

LONG. (General) Usually refers to a ball which, due to english and stroke, travels a path with wider angles than those that are standard for such a ball if struck with natural english and moderate speed.

LONG STRING. (Pocket games) A line drawn from the center of the foot cushion to the foot spot (and beyond if necessary) on which balls are spotted.

LOSING HAZARD. (Snooker) Occurs when the cue ball is pocketed after contact with an object ball.

LOT. (General) Procedures used, not involving billiard skills, to determine starting player or order of play in casual or non-tournament play. Common methods used are flipping coins, drawing straws, drawing cards, or drawing peas or pills.

MASSE SHOT. (General) A shot in which extreme *english* is applied to the cue ball by means of elevating the cue butt at an angle with the bed of the table of anywhere between 30 and 90 degrees.

MECHANICAL BRIDGE. (General) A grooved device mounted on a handle providing support for the shaft of the cue during shots difficult to reach with normal bridge hand. Also called a "crutch" or "rake."

MISCUE. (General) A stroke which results in the cue tip contact with cue ball being faulty. Usually the cue tip slides off the cue ball without full transmission of the desired stroke.

MISS. (General) Failure to execute a completed shot.

NATURAL. (Carom games) A shot with only natural angle and stroke required for successful execution; a simple or easily visualized, and accomplished, scoring opportunity.

NATURAL ENGLISH. (General) Moderate sidespin applied to the cue ball that favors the direction of the cue ball path, giving the cue ball a natural roll and a bit more speed than a center hit.

NATURAL ROLL. (General) Movement of the cue ball with no *english* applied.

NIP DRAW. (General) A short, sharp stroke, employed when a normal *draw* stroke would result in a foul due to drawing the cue ball back into the cue tip.

NURSES. (Carom games) Techniques whereby the balls are kept close to the cushions and each other, creating a succession of relatively easy scoring opportunities.

OBJECT BALLS. (General) The balls other than the cue ball on a shot.

OBJECT BALL, THE (Pocket games) The particular object ball being played on a shot.

ON BALL. (Snooker) See *ball on.*

OPEN BREAK. (Pocket games) The requirement in certain games that a player must drive a minimum of four object balls out of the *rack* to the cushions in order for the shot to be legal.

OPENING BREAK SHOT. (General) The first shot of a game.

PEAS. (Pocket games) Small plastic balls numbered 1 through 15 or 16, use defined in specific game rules. (Also called *pills.*)

PILLS. (Pocket games) see *peas.*

PLANT. (Snooker) A position of two or more red balls that allows a ball to be driven into a pocket with a *combination* shot.

POSITION. (General) The placement of the cue ball on each shot relative to the next planned shot.

POWDER. (General) Talc or other fine, powdery substance used to facilitate free, easy movement of the cue shaft through the *bridge.*

POWER DRAW SHOT. (General) Extreme *draw* applied to the cue ball. (Also see *force draw*.)

PUSH SHOT. (General) A shot in which the cue tip maintains contact with the cue ball beyond the split second allowed for a normal and legally stroked shot.

PYRAMID. (Pocket games) Positioning of the object balls in a triangular grouping (with the front apex ball on the foot spot), used to begin many pocket billiard games.

RACE. (General) Pre-determined number of games necessary to win a match or set of games.

RAILS. (General) The top surface of the table, not covered by cloth, from which the cushions protrude toward the playing surface. The head and foot rails are the short rails on those ends of the table; the right and left rails are the long rails, dictated by standing at the head end of the table and facing the foot end.

RED BALL. (Carom games) The red-colored object ball. (Also the name of a particular 3-cushion billiard game.)

REVERSE ENGLISH. (General) Sidespin applied to the cue ball, that favors the opposite direction of the natural cue ball path, which causes it to rebound from an object ball or a cushion at a slower speed than it would if struck at the same speed and direction without *english*.

ROUND ROBIN. (General) A tournament format in which each contestant plays each of the other players once.

RUNNING ENGLISH. (General) Sidespin applied to the cue ball which causes it to rebound from an object ball or a cushion at a more acute angle and at a faster speed than it would if struck at the same speed and direction without *english*.

RUN. (General) The total of consecutive scores, points or counts made by a player in one *inning*. The term is also used to indicate the total number of full short-rack games won without a missed shot in a match or tournament.

SAFETY. (General) Defensive positioning of the balls so as to minimize the opponent's chances to score. (The nature and rules concerning safety play are decidedly different in specific games; see individual game rules regarding safety play.) Player's inning ends after a safety play.

SCRATCH. (Carom games) To score a point largely by accident, due to an unanticipated kiss, unplanned time-shot, etc.

SCRATCH. (Pocket games) The cue ball going into a pocket on a stroke.

SEEDING. (General) Pre-determined initial pairings or advanced positioning of players in a field of tournament competition.

SET. (General) Pre-determined number of games necessary to win a match.

SHAFT. (General) The thinner part of a cue, on which the cue tip is attached. On a two-piece cue, the shaft extends from the *cue tip* to the *joint*.

SHAKE BOTTLE. (Pocket games) See *bottle*.

SHORT. (General) Usually refers to a ball which, due to stroke, travels a path with more narrow angles than those that are standard for a ball struck without *english*.

SHORT-RACK. (Pocket games) Games which utilize less than 15 object balls.

SINGLE ELIMINATION. (General) A tournament format in which a single loss eliminates a player from the competition.

SNAKE. (Carom games) A shot in which the use of *english* causes the cue ball to make three or more cushion contacts, though utilizing only two different cushions.

SNOOKERBED. (Snooker) The condition of incoming player's cue ball position when he cannot shoot in a straight line and contact all portions of an *on ball* directly facing the cue ball (because of balls not "on" that block the path). (Included for information only, since the rules of American Snooker in this book are of such nature that being snookered has no special impact on the game rules or play).

SPLIT DOUBLE ELIMINATION. (General) A modification of the *double elimination* tournament format, in which the field is divided into sections, with one player emerging from each of the sections to compete for the championship, in a single showdown match for the championship.

SPOT. (General) The thin, circular piece of cloth or paper glued onto the cloth to indicate the spot locals (i.e., head spot, center spot, foot spot); also an expression to describe a handicap.

SPOT BALL. (Carom games) The white ball differentiated from the clear by one or more markings; usually spots, dots or circles.

SPOT SHOT. (Pocket games) Player shoots a ball on the foot spot with the cue ball in hand behind the head string.

SPOTTING BALLS. (General) Replacing balls to the table in positions as dictated by specific game rules.

STANCE. (General) The position of the body during shooting. (See **Instructional Playing Tips.**)

STOP SHOT. (Pocket games) A shot in which the cue ball stops immediately upon striking the object ball.

STROKE. (General) The movement of the cue as a shot is executed. (See **Instructional Playing Tips.**)

SUCCESSIVE FOULS. (Pocket games) Fouls made on consecutive strokes by the same player, also called consecutive fouls.

TABLE IN POSITION. (General) Term used to indicate that the object balls remain unmoved following a shot.

THROW SHOT. (Pocket games) 1. A *cut shot* that alters the path of the ball by applying *english*. 2. A combination shot of frozen or near frozen object balls that is struck by the cue ball left or right of center on the first object ball, thus causing the second (or played) object ball to travel in the opposite direction of the cue ball hit.

TIME SHOT. (General) A shot in which the cue ball (most often) moves another ball into a different position and then continues on to meet one of the transposed balls for a score.

TRIANGLE. (Pocket games) The triangular device used to place the balls in position for the start of most games.

INSTRUCTIONAL PLAYING TIPS

By Jerry Briesath, Richard Rhorer

There are many variations of the game of billiards, but the fundamentals of good billiard playing are inherent in every format of the sport. This section deals with these fundamentals.

CUE SELECTION: Try several cues and start with one that feels most comfortable to you. It is difficult for a beginning pool player to know which weight of a cue to get. Keep in mind that most professional pool players use a cue that is between 18 to 20 ounces. The shaft size of a cue mainly has to do with personal preference and the size of your fingers. Shaft sizes for pool cues basically run between 12 to 14 millimeters. Most professional pool players play with a shaft size of $12^{1}/_{2}$ to $13^{1}/_{2}$ mm.

PROPER GRIP OF A CUE:
Hold the cue lightly with the thumb and first three fingers. (See Figure #1). When the cue is gripped properly, it should not touch the palm of your hand. (See Figure #2). It is very important to maintain a light grip on the cue at all times. Gripping the cue too tightly while stroking through the cue ball is a common mistake that must be corrected.

Figure No. 1   Figure No. 2

WHERE TO GRIP THE CUE: When you are bent over in your shooting position and the cue tip is almost touching the cue ball, the shooting hand should be directly under the elbow. It is okay to have the shooting hand an inch or two ahead of the elbow at impact. It is never recommended to have the shooting hand behind the elbow at impact. (See Figure #3).

Figure No. 3

The following Instructions and Illustrations are for Right Handed Players

CUE STANCE: Face the shot. Before you even bend over to shoot, there is a line up of three points - the chin, the cue ball and the exact place you want the cue ball to go. Turn your body slightly to the right without your chin leaving the point of line up. Bend over at the waist, put your bridge hand down seven to ten inches from the cue ball so that your chin is 2 to 8 inches directly above the cue stick. Adjust your feet to distribute your body weight approximately 50/50 (as shown in Figure #4). When in your shooting position, a generally accepted stance is when the tip of the right toe is directly under the line of the cue and the left toe is slightly to the left side of the line of the cue. This should allow a four to six inch gap between the hip and the cue for freedom of movement.

Figure No. 4

A common mistake made by beginners in their shooting position is having the shoulders and chest facing the cue ball. A preferred technique is to turn the left shoulder out in front and the right shoulder back thus turning the chest more to the right. This makes a more proper body alignment. (See Figure #5).

Figure No. 5

BRIDGES: One of the most overlooked fundamentals of the game is a solid bridge. The difference between a good billiard player and just another billiard player can most often be traced to their bridge. Nothing is of greater importance in billiard play. If the shot you are executing is to be accurate, your bridge must be natural, yet give firm guidance to the cue. Adapt the following formulas for your correct bridges. There are two basic bridges–an open bridge and a closed bridge.

Figure No. 6

Open Bridge: An open bridge is one formed by placing the hand firmly on the table, cupping the hand, pressing the thumb against the forefinger forming a "V". (See Figure #6). The cue is now placed on the "V" (See Figure #7). To adjust the height of the bridge, simply pull the fingers toward you raising the bridge (See Figure #8), or pushing the fingers away to lower the bridge (See Figure #9). This allows you to strike the cue ball high, medium or low while maintaining a solid bridge. This bridge is highly recommended for

Figure No. 7

Figure No. 8

Figure No. 9

beginners. Professionals use this bridge on many shots that don't require a lot of power or cue ball spin.

Stretch Shots: When stretching out for a shot where a long bridge is required (12 inches or more), it is very important to use an open bridge. Keep the back swing and follow through very short and use minimum speed. (See Figure #10).

Closed Bridge: Place your entire bridge hand flat on the table. The heel of your hand should be down firmly (See Figure #11). Bend your forefinger so that its tip touches your thumb, thus forming a loop (See Figure #12). Place the cue tip in the loop formed by forefinger

Figure No. 10

and thumb, resting the cue against the inner groove of these two fingers. Extend

Figure No. 11

Figure No. 12

Figure No. 13

the cue through the loop formed by the above. Now pull your forefinger firmly against the cue, but with the loop just loose enough so that you can stroke the cue back and forth easily. As you do the above, keep your middle, ring and small finger spread out and firmly pressed against the table. They form the bridge tripod which must be firm, yet natural. You have the correct bridge when the cue passes through easily, accurately and with firm guidance and support.

The bridge length   is the distance between the loop of the forefinger and the cue ball on a closed bridge or the thumb and the cue ball on an open bridge. Most professional pool players use a bridge length of 7 to 10 inches. Whether you use an open or a closed bridge, the heel of your hand should be firmly on the table at all times. The bridge hand must not move while you are striking the ball.

Bridge for Follow Shot: Using a Standard Bridge, elevate the tripod fingers slightly. Keep the cue level (See Figure #13).

Bridge for Draw Shot: Using the Standard Bridge, lower the tripod fingers until your thumb rests on the bed of the table. Keep the cue level (See Figure #14).

Figure No. 14

Rail Bridges: If the cue ball is four inches or more away from the rail, set your bridge hand on the rail. Place your thumb under the index finger. (See Figure #15). Put the cue on the rail against the thumb, and bring your forefinger over the shaft (See Figure #16). Keep your cue as level as possible when stroking your shot.

If the cue ball is closer than four inches of the rail, place the cue between the thumb and forefinger. Place the other three fingers on the rail (as shown in Figure #17).

Figure No. 15   Figure No. 16

Bridge for Over Ball Shot: When it is necessary to shoot over an object ball in order to stroke the cue ball, the following bridge should be employed. Bracing all four of your fingers on the bed of the table behind the obstructing object ball(s), raise the hand as high as necessary and place the cue on the support made by your index finger joint and the thumb (See Figures #18

Figure No. 17

& #19). This is an uncomfortable bridge, but a very necessary one, which should be practiced.

Figure No. 18

Figure No. 19

Mechanical Bridges: If a shot is beyond reach with any of the above mentioned bridges, a mechanical bridge should be employed. Don't sacrifice a shot because you cannot use the mechanical bridge; it is very easy. Set the bridge on the table 6 to 8 inches from the cue ball. Place your hand on the bridge. Place the shaft of your cue in the notch at the front part of the bridge. (Use higher notch for "follow," lower notch for "draw" or "stop.") Place your thumb under the base of the cue and your four fingers over the top of the cue. Your elbow will be sticking out to the side as you stroke; the bridge will be to the left if you are right-handed. Be sure to lay the bridge flat on the table if possible (See Figure #20) and secure it with your left hand. Now use the same system as for any other shot.

Figure No. 20

LEARNING A STROKE

Remember, "Practice doesn't make Perfect; *Perfect Practice* makes Perfect." A stroke is a throwing motion. A good throwing motion starts with a slow backswing with a smooth acceleration through the cue ball. A common mistake by amateur and beginning players is to drop the elbow while stroking through the cue ball. It's important to note that the *throwing* motion must only take place in that part of the arm below the elbow. The less the elbow moves up and down, the more precise the stroke. It should be a pendulum swing from the elbow down.

CUEING THE BALL

For the beginning player, it is important to adjust the bridge so that the cue tip strikes the cue ball a little above center, never to the left or right, while he is learning accuracy and speed control. As his skill level progresses, it will be necessary for him to learn to strike the cue ball at other places–higher, lower, left, right, etc.

The most important three things to learn after a player has progressed past the beginner stage are (1) how to make the cue ball follow (2) how to stop your cue ball on a straight in shot and (3) how to make the cue ball draw or reverse direction off the object ball (See Figure #21 for further details). The smoother the stroke, the lower or higher the cue ball may be struck without miscueing. Most good players can strike the cue ball almost two full tips off center without miscueing.

Keep in mind that extreme spin requires a very good stroke and smooth

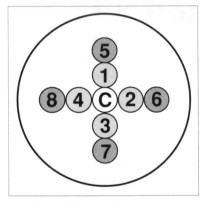

delivery. When following the cue ball, the higher the tip strikes the cue ball, the more overspin will be pushed on the cue ball; likewise for backspin. The lower you shoot the cue ball, the more spin is imparted to the cue ball by the cue tip. In pool there is one stroke. You use the same stroke to follow the ball as you do to stop or draw the cue ball.

A common mistake for people is that when they want to stop or draw the cue ball, they think they have to *jab* or hit the cue ball and stop the cue tip immediately on impact with the cue ball or even hit the cue ball and pull the stick back. That is not

Figure No. 21

the way to stop or draw the cue ball. To make the cue ball stop, you must put enough back spin on it by shooting below center to cause it to arrive at the object ball with no spin. The cloth is always trying to rub the back spin off the cue ball. The farther the cue ball is from the object ball, the lower and/or harder you must shoot to cause the cue ball to stop or come back (Figure #21 shows positions 1-4 and also 5-8 extreme spin). When using back spin on the cue ball, it is important to understand the concept that the back spin you put on the cue ball is caused by the tremendous friction the chalk creates between the tip and the cue ball. You must understand that the cue stick pushes back spin on the cue ball as you *throw* it 4 to 6 inches through the lower part of the cue ball. (Figure #22 shows how the cue stick follows through 4 to 6 inches after contact with the object ball).

HITTING THE OBJECT BALL

The first thing the pocket billiard player must learn is that his eyes should be on the object ball as he executes the shot. During the aiming process his eyes go back and forth between the cue ball and the object ball. When you are ready to pocket the object ball, your eyes are on the object ball.

Figure No. 22

To shoot a ball into a pocket, the simplest way to determine your point of impact on the object ball is to draw an imaginary line from the center of the pocket which bisects the object ball. Where this line extends through the object ball is your contact point. It is the point at which the edge of the cue ball must contact the edge of the object ball. You must aim so that these two contact points will meet (See Figure #23).

Figure No. 23

Figure No. 24

Figure No. 25

POINT OF AIM, POINT OF IMPACT

In Figures #24 & #25, you can see there is a white dot on the object ball. This mark is where the cue ball must contact the object ball in order to pocket the ball. The white dot is called the Point of Impact. The white dot on the table is the Point of Aim. No matter where the cue ball is the cue stick and the center of the cue ball are aimed at the Point of Aim in order to contact the Point of Impact on the object ball.

A keen eye and judgement are important here. Your skill in hitting the point of aim will determine your status in pocket billiard circles.

Once again there is no better experience than practice. Accomplish this phase by placing your cue ball close to the object ball, then gradually increase the distance between the two balls. Time and practice will increase your accuracy in striking the cue ball correctly and hitting the object ball where you aim, thus driving it to the exact target area desired.

LEARNING A GOOD SHOOTING SYSTEM

The first thing you have to remember when you play pool is that you don't control the balls. All you control is your body and your cue stick. What the balls do is only a result of how well your body moves the cue stick. There are two things you have to get out of the way before you can shoot any shot. You have to make sure the cue is aiming straight and you have to make sure your arm can move the cue straight back and forth the full length of your bridge (7 to 10 inches).

A good practice technique for this is to place the cue ball on the spot and shoot it down the table into a corner pocket. Be sure to get your stance and aim correct. Then take a couple of smooth, slow warm-up swings the full length of the bridge. Stop at the cue ball and check your aim by letting your eyes go down the line of the cue stick to the target and back a couple of times. If the aim looks perfect, lock your eyes on the target, then after a slow backswing, "throw" the cue stick smoothly 4 to 6 inches through the cue ball directly over the dot. If after executing the shot, the cue stick is to the left or right of the dot, repeat this system until you can shoot the ball into the pocket and the cue stick finishes it's motion 4 to 6 inches straight ahead and directly over the dot. It is *imperative* that the head remain perfectly still during the shot. This is an important practice to help in developing your accuracy and stroke.

The warm-up swings should be slow and smooth in both directions training the arm to make the cue go straight. After every two or three warm-up strokes, be sure to stop the cue ball and check the aim. If it looks perfect, take a smooth backswing, and then accelerate 4 to 6 inches through the cue ball at any speed you want to shoot. It is very important that you always maintain the same slow backswing no matter how hard you accelerate through the ball. Never go back faster just because you want to shoot harder. It's just like throwing a ball, to be accurate, you go back slowly, then you throw hard.

It is important to learn to stroke through the ball at all speeds. Although you have more control at slower speeds, sometimes position play will require you to shoot a ball harder. Keep in mind–slow backswing, accelerate forward.

ENGLISH (Left or Right)

When we talk about *english*, we are generally referring to left or right spin on the cue ball. By putting left or right spin on the cue ball, you immediately do three things that can cause you to miss a shot. Beginning with right hand english, when you strike the cue ball on the right hand side, the cue ball (1) immediately deflects off the tip to the left of the line of the cue stick. As the cue ball proceeds down the table, it may (2) curve back to the right just a little bit. It will never curve back as much as it deflects unless you elevate the cue, which we're not going to talk about here. With a level cue and right hand english on the ball, it will first deflect to the left. It might curve back a little to the right depending on the distance. The third thing is that the english might *throw* the object ball. Right hand english can throw the object ball a little to the left of the contact line. The curve back is dependent on the speed and the distance that the cue ball is traveling.

We mention three things that happen when you use right hand english, the deflection immediately off the tip, the curve back to the right and the throwing the object ball to the left. Of these three, the curve is usually very slight. The throwing of the object ball is very slight. The biggest factor in causing people to miss with english is the *deflection* off the cue tip. It is important to remember when using right hand english, aim slightly to the right of where you would normally aim on the object ball. When using left hand english, you must aim slightly to the left of where you would normally aim on the object ball.

Left or right hand english is almost never used to pocket an object ball; but rather for playing position on another object ball. The purpose of applying sidespin to the cue ball is to change the angle at which the cue ball comes off a rail after pocketing the object ball. Always remember never use english to make balls, *only* to play position on the next ball. Although english is extremely important in playing position, the pros will tell you 'the less english you use the less often you get in trouble.' (See Chart A).

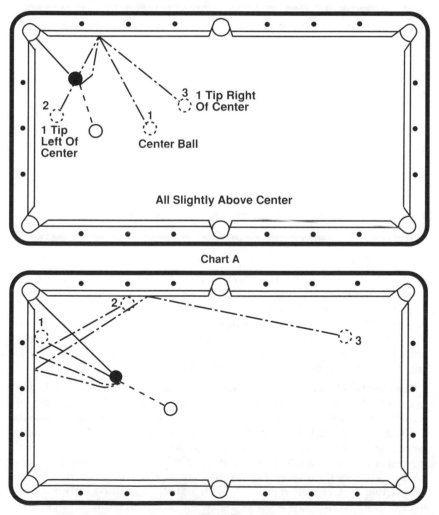

Chart A

Chart B

Follow Shots: Set up the balls as in Chart B. By stroking the cue ball between a tip and a tip and a half above center, the cue ball will follow to Position 1. Then set up the same shot and stroke the cue ball at the same height, add some power and see that the cue ball will end up in Position 2. Now stroke the cue ball again in the same position, but with an even firmer stroke to see the cue ball respond as in Postition 3 on the Diagram.

Stop Shots: Place the balls on the table as in Chart C. Strike the cue ball about a tip below center. Use a smooth stroke and practice stopping the cue ball as it contacts the object ball. Do this a few times to get the feel of how hard you shoot, then practice shooting this same shot a little lower on the cue ball with a little less speed and see if you can still get the same results. Then proceed to Postition 2. This

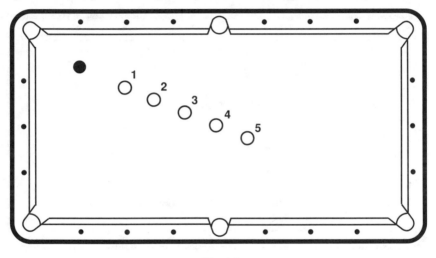

Chart C

time stroke the cue ball about a tip and a half below center and a little firmer than Position 1. By repeating this practice in a new position, you will learn how much force you need in order to stop the cue ball. Continue this practice with the cue ball in Postitions 3 & 4 each time increasing the power of the stroke. If you have any difficulty at a particular position, repeat that practice until it feels comfortable. Remember, the lower you strike the cue ball, the less power is required to stop the cue ball on contact with the object ball.

Draw Shots: Place the balls as shown in Chart D. Notice there is a *slight* angle in the ball placement so that when you draw the cue ball it will move over to the right slightly and then come back past your cue stick. The reason for this is so that you can follow through the cue ball 4 to 6 inches to practice a good follow through on each shot without worrying about the cue ball hitting your stick. With the balls in position, strike the cue ball about a tip and a half below center with a moderate stroke and notice that the cue ball travels a couple of inches to the right of your stick before it travels a short distance down the table to Position 1. By increasing the force of your stroke, you will be able to move the ball farther down the table

Chart D

toward Positions 2 & 3. It is important on all these exercises to be sure the cue tip follows through 4 to 6 inches. If you shoot the cue ball for any stop or draw shot, the cue ball is struck one to one and a half tips below center. When the pendelum motion of the arm is correct, the cue tip will follow through 4 to 6 inches past the object ball, and continue in a slightly downward motion, ending up touching the cloth.

Position Play: Players are forever trying to play position. That is making an easy shot and making the cue ball arrrive at a place on the table to have another easy shot. The two secrets of playing proper position are (1) memory and (2) speed control. When a beginner is learning to play, he should repeat the same shots over and over. Not only do you watch the object ball being pocketed, but the path of the cue ball after contacting the object ball. If you are continually hitting the object ball a little above center, the cue ball will always take virtually the same path. Fifty percent of position play is remembering where the cue ball went after that particular shot. The other fifty percent of position play is the speed control of the cue ball.

The most important and easiest way a beginner can learn position is to set up a shot (as in Chart E). When you set up a practice shot, mark the cloth with a dot of chalk under the object ball and the cue ball, so you start at the same position each time. Pocket the object ball by hitting it a little above center and watch where the cue ball hits the first rail and the direction it takes coming off that rail. By shooting this shot several times at different speeds, but striking the cue ball in the same spot each time, you will notice the path of the cue ball will follow in almost the same line each time you shoot. To improve your game, work on playing position on each of the shots in the diagram by varying the speed in which you strike the cue ball.

Now if you set the balls up in the same position and strike the cue ball a little below center, you will notice that the path of the cue ball will be completely different off the object ball. Repeat this several times, until you can make the cue

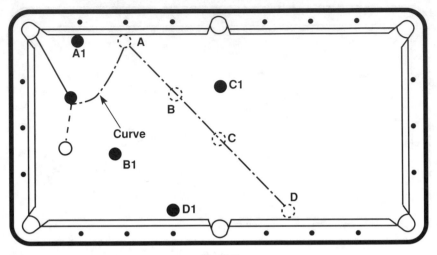

Chart E

ball go in the same direction, but travel farther down the table depending on the speed of your stroke. After setting up these shots and executing them by hitting the ball a little below center, set them up again and strike the cue ball even farther below center. This is a good exercise to learn the basics of what happens when you shoot the cue ball at different heights and speeds.

EXERCISES

FOLLOW, STOP AND DRAW: This exercise is to show you the different ways the cue ball will react when it is cued at different levels. Set up the shot in Chart F. The object ball is about a diamond out and directly inline between the two side pockets. The cue ball is at a slight angle toward the diamond past the side pocket.

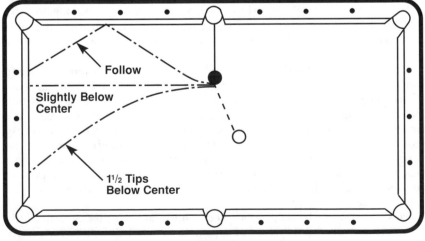

Chart F

When you hit the cue ball with follow, the cue ball will take a slight curve as shown in the path in the diagram. If you hit the cue ball slightly below center, it will go almost straight down the table. If the cue ball is hit about one and a half tips below center, it will curve back more toward the corner pocket.

POSITION EXERCISE: Learning Position Play is learning the easiest way to get the balls off the table. The best way to learn that is an exercise we call 3-Ball, Ball in Hand. This is one of the best exercises to improve your skill level in control and position. Throw 3 balls on the table. In chart G, we see balls 1, 2 and 3. This numeric order is the easiest way to play off these balls by placing the cue ball as shown. Striking the cue ball above center on the #1 ball, you can see by the path of the cue ball that it will follow into the rail and then head right toward the #2 ball. By going to the rail after pocketing the #1 ball and depending on your speed of stroke, you can end up in any of the three cue ball positions. It is very difficult to make a mistake. This is what pros look for: The easiest way to get position on their next ball. If you shoot the cue ball again above center and pocket the #2 ball, the

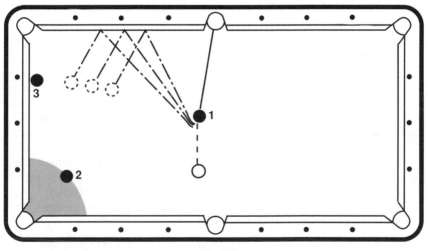

Chart G

cue ball ends up anywhere within the darkened circle around the #2 ball. Then the #3 ball is an easily pocketed shot.

One of the best ways of improving your game of pool is by repeating shots. Don't repeat long, difficult shots. The ones to repeat are the easy and semi-easy ones that are frequently missed. For the more proficient players, even if you make the object ball and fail to get position, repeat that same shot until you feel comfortable that you can make that ball and get position.

Most people think that if they could make tough shots, they would be better players. The reality is that games are not won by people that make the tough shots; games are lost by players that miss shots that are very easy.

Chart H shows the many ways the speed of stroke can be used to play position. By using a soft stroke, you can play shape to position "A" to play "A1" for your next shot. A slightly harder stroke will go to position "B" for "B1" as the next shot.

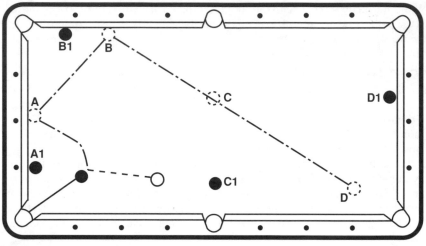

Chart H

Continue working on your speed of stroke until you can play position on shots "C1" & "D1".

8-BALL AND 9-BALL, BALL IN HAND: Another great practice technique for beginners or stronger players is to play 8-Ball or 9-Ball with a rule change. When a person breaks and a ball is made on the break, he can take "Ball in Hand" anywhere on the table and shoot until he misses. The incoming player also takes "ball in hand" and shoots until he misses. The advantage of playing this way is that when you have ball in hand every time you come to the table, you start looking over the table. Even a beginner will start to see patterns of two or maybe three balls. The better player learns very quickly the easiest way to run the balls off. It trains you to see patterns and see the easy way to go for a run out. By playing Ball in Hand pool whether it is 8-Ball or 9-Ball, you learn in one hour the equivalent of what you would learn in about 15 hours of regular practice.

BALL IN HAND EQUAL OFFENSE: Another great practice game is a variation of Equal Offense which is also in this book. In Equal Offense each ball is one point and you can shoot at any ball. No balls count on the break. After the break, the same player that breaks, gets ball in hand three times per rack. After each miss, he gets ball in hand again. Then he records how many balls he made that rack. A perfect score is 150 points in 10 racks. By playing this 3 miss way, a person learns to see and play simple patterns. When a person's score approaches 130 or more in ten racks, then he progresses to the "2-Miss" level. Now he breaks the balls and after the break, he gets ball in hand twice per rack. When his score improves again to 130 or more in ten racks, then he is playing well enough to progress to the one miss level. Any player that shoots 130 points or more on the "1-Miss" level, is a very good amateur player. This is a great practice game.

THROW SHOTS: (Charts I, J, K, L) The object of a "throw" shot is to provide force or english that will move an object ball along an off-center path, when two balls are *frozen*.

This situation often arises when the cue ball is touching (frozen) to an object ball. If the two are in alignment with a pocket, there is no problem. If not in alignment, it is still possible to pocket the object ball by using a "throw shot" which spins the object ball to the left or right. Chart I shows how, by hitting the cue ball on the left side, the object ball is thrown to the right side. Chart J illustrates that striking the cue ball on the right side moves the object ball to the left.

Another version of the throw shot is when two object balls are frozen together. The cue ball is free, but not in position to pocket either ball easily. In this case, the cue ball (hit without english) strikes the closest object ball on either the right

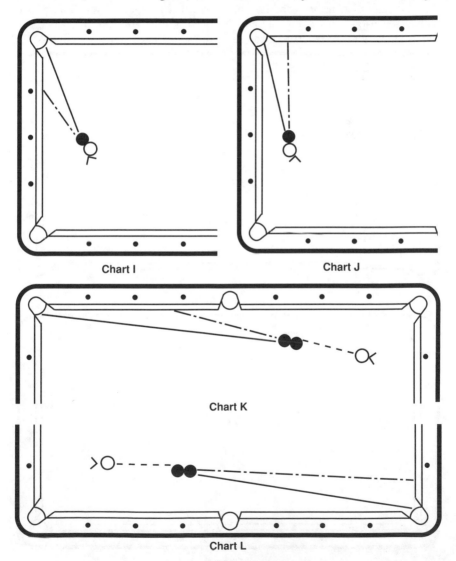

Chart I

Chart J

Chart K

Chart L

side (Chart K) or the left side (Chart L) to throw the second object ball in the opposite direction.

Kiss Shots: (Chart M & N) The object of this exercise is to pocket one of two balls that are frozen together without the use of english. When two balls are frozen together, an axis or center line is established by their relationship. A cue extended along this imaginary line will readily determine if the closest object ball, when struck on the back half, will follow the line into a pocket. If the cue does not point to a pocket, the object ball will not go into a pocket.

Chart M shows how this kiss shot can be made from either side. Chart N demonstrates that one object ball can be pocketed. The other cannot. Arrange two balls into various frozen positions and practice finding the center line. Then, mix throw shots with kiss shots to increase your options under these conditions.

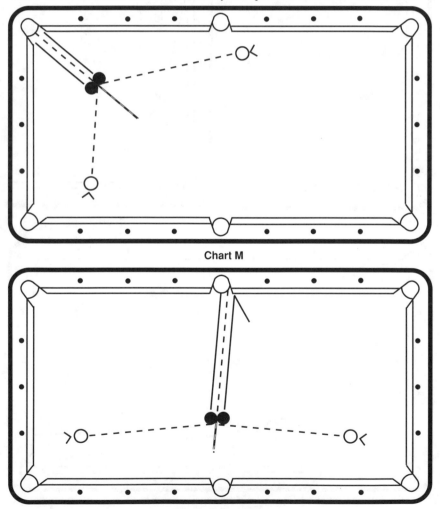

Chart M

Chart N

RULES FOR TOURNAMENT PLAY

The following rules concern the play, scoring, officiating and responsibilities for tournament competition in both pocket and carom games. However, the precepts and principles of these rules are to be considered part of the games' General Rules, and should be applied as appropriate to all play, whether or not a formal tournament.

It is the player's responsibility to be aware of all rules, regulations and schedules applying to his competition. While tournament officials will make every reasonable effort to have such information readily available to all players as appropriate, the ultimate responsibility rests with the player himself. Though referees may do their best to advise all players of certain traditional and factual situations during play (such as being "on two fouls" in **14.1**, or being "on one" or "on two fouls" in **Nine Ball**), once again the player has no recourse if such information is not volunteered; the responsibility for knowing his situation and/ or the rules lies with the player himself.

ACCEPTANCE OF EQUIPMENT. Tournament players should assure themselves, prior to beginning play, that the balls and other equipment are standard and legal. Once they begin play of a match, they may no longer question the legality of the equipment in use (unless the opponent **and** tournament officials both agree with the objection **and** any available remedy proposed by the tournament officials).

USE OF EQUIPMENT. Players may not use equipment or accessory items for purposes or in a manner other than those for which the items were intended. For example, powder containers, chalk cubes, etc., may not be used to prop up a *mechanical bridge* (or natural hand bridge); no more than two mechanical bridges may be used at one time; nor may they be used to support anything other than the *cue shaft*. Extra or out-of-play balls may not be used by players to check clearances or for any other reason (except to lag for break); the triangle may not be employed by players to ascertain whether a ball is in the rack **unless** a match is unofficiated and the table has not been pencil-marked around the triangle area.

Tournament officials should prevent these actions from occuring. Generally, no penalty is applied, because the referee or other tournament official intercedes prior to that point. However, should a player persist in activity counter to this (or any other) general rule after having been advised that the activity is not permissable, tournament officials may take action against him as appropriate under the provisions of "Unsportsmanlike Conduct."

EQUIPMENT RESTRICTIONS. Players may use chalk, powder, mechanical bridge(s) and cue of their choice and/or design. However, tournament officials may restrict a player if he attempts action that is disruptive of either the house equipment or normal competitive conditions. As examples, a player may be restrained from using blue chalk on gold cloth; he may be advised not to use powder in such an excessive fashion as to unduly affect the balls or table cloth; he may be barred from using a cue with a noise-making device that is clearly disruptive to other competitors.

MARKING OF TABLES. Prior to competition, each table and the triangle to be used on it shall be marked so as to ensure that the same triangle will be used throughout the tournament on the same table.

An accurate and clearly visible pencil line must also be marked on the cloth: (1) around the outer edge of the triangle to ensure accurate and consistent placement to enable accurate judgement as to ball positions; (2) on the long string to enable accurate spotting of balls; and (3) on the head string to facilitate determinations of whether balls are behind the head string.

The *head spot, center spot* and *foot spot* must also be determined to be accurately marked, whether with discreet penciled "plus" marks, or with standard spots if being employed.

ILLEGALLY CAUSING BALL TO MOVE. Any player who, in the referee's judgement, **intentionally** causes a ball to move by any illegal means (pushing on bed cloth, bumping or slapping table, etc.) will lose the game and/or match by forfeit. (Referee's judgement and discretion under "Unsportsmanlike Conduct").

ADMINISTRATIVE DISCRETION. The management of each tournament shall reserve the right to set forth rules and procedures appropriate and reasonable for the particular tournament involved, such as may regard players' dress requirements, method or receiving entry fees, refund policy of entry fees, scheduling flexibility, pairing procedures, etc.

However, for tournaments to receive a BCA sanction, certain requirements must be met, primarily with regard to safeguarding and ensuring proper distribution of the prize fund. (See **BCA Tournament Sanctioning**.)

TOURNAMENT OFFICIALS/REFEREES. Where these rules refer to a "referee," it should be noted that the referees' perogatives and discretion also accrue to other tournament officials as appropriate.

REFEREE'S AUTHORITY. The referee is in complete charge of the match he is officiating. He may, at his discretion, consult other tournament officials for rule interpretations, ball positions, etc. However, all matters of judgement are his and his alone; they cannot be appealed to higher tournament authority by players; only if the referee is in error on a rule or its application, may higher tournament authority overrule him.

REFEREE'S RESPONSIVENESS. The referee shall be totally responsive to players' inquiries regarding objective data, such as whether a ball will be in the rack, if a ball is in the kitchen, what the count is, how many points are needed for a victory, if a player is playing from safety, if a player or his opponent is on a foul, what rule would apply if a certain shot is made etc. However, he must not offer or provide any subjective opinion that would affect play, such as whether a good hit can be made on a prospective shot, whether a combination is makeable, how the table seems to be playing etc.

FINAL TOURNAMENT AUTHORITY. Though these rules attempt to cover the vast majority of situations that arise in competition, there still may be an occasional need for interpretation of the rules and their proper application under unusual circumstances. The Tournament Director or other official who assumes final responsibility for a tournament will make any such required decision (other than referee's judgement calls) at his discretion, and they shall be final.

WAGERING BY REFEREES. Referees are strictly prohibited from any wagering of any kind involving the games, players or tournament in any way. Any such wagering by a referee (or other tournament official) shall result in his immediate dismissal and the forfeiture of his entire financial compensation for the tournament.

SCORING OF FORFEITS. Matches forfeited for any reason under these rules shall not result in any scores being included in the statistics of a tournament, regardless of whether any score had been reached prior to the declaration of forfeiture. For official records, no point scores should be recorded, but rather the notations "W(F)" and "L(F)" as appropriate should be employed. (Matches lost through disqualification are considered forfeits for purposes of this rule.)

If, however, the player awarded a match through his opponent's forfeiture has posted a high run (or similar accomplishment for which an award is granted) during play of the match prior to declaration of forfeiture, that high run or other mark shall be eligible for the tournament award or prize.

(NOTE: U.S.B.A. 3-Cushion Rules differ; see specific game rules.)

OUT OF HEAD STRING WARNING. When player has the *cue ball in hand behind the head string*, the referee shall warn him before he shoots if he has not placed it within the head string. If the player shoots on or outside the string after having been warned of the legal placement, the stroke is a foul. See specific game rules for penalty.

REMAINING IN PLAYER'S CHAIR. Players are to remain in the chair designated for their use while opponent is at the table. Should a player need to leave the playing area during matches, he must request and receive permission from the referee. The referee shall apply his good judgement to ensure that undue time is not being used or that a player is not abusing the privilege as a means of unsettling an opponent.

OUTSIDE ASSISTANCE PROHIBITED. Unless specifically permitted by the rules of a given tournament, players may not knowingly accept any form of playing advice during a match. A player may not engage in communication, either verbal or nonverbal, with persons other than the tournament officials or his opponent during play.

Should a player desire to so communicate, for example to obtain a beverage, get a piece of equipment, or other permissable reason, he should either communicate through a tournament official or with the approval and observance of the referee.

If the referee has reason to believe that a player knowingly solicited or accepted outside assistance in any manner regarding the play of a match, he shall take steps appropriate under the provisions of "Unsportsmanlike Conduct."

NON-PLAYER INTERFERENCE OR HARASSMENT. If a non-player either verbally or visually interferes with the players, the referee may request that he leave the playing area.

PROTESTS. A player may request a rule interpretation or application from the referee or appropriate tournament authority. He must, however, make such a request or protest immediately, prior to any subsequent shot being taken, or it cannot be considered or honored.

All players must honor an opponent's request that play be halted if an official is to be summoned or if a referee is to check or verify a rule question with other officials. Failure to honor such requests may result in disqualification or forfeiture under the provisions of "Unsportsmanlike Conduct."

UNSPORTSMANLIKE CONDUCT. The referee has the right and obligation to ensure that no player engages in any activity which, in his judgement, is unsportsmanlike in nature, embarrassing, disruptive or detrimental to other players, tournament officials or hosts, or the sport in general. The referee or other officials shall have the right to penalize or disqualify, with or without warning, any player who conducts himself in an unsportsmanlike manner.

GENERAL RULES OF POCKET BILLIARDS

The rules included in this section are those that apply generally to all the specific varieties of pocket billiard games included in this rulebook. These general rules apply to all pocket billiard games, UNLESS specifically noted to the contrary in the individual game rules.

To facilitate the use and understanding of these general rules, terms that may require definition are set in *italics* so that the reader may refer to the **Glossary of Billiard Terms** section for the exact meaning of the term.

For purposes of simplicity and clarity, masculine pronouns have been utilized throughout this rulebook. Such references apply to any player or teams of players.

1. TABLES, BALLS, EQUIPMENT. All games described in this rulebook are designed for tables, balls and equipment meeting the standards prescribed in the **"BCA Equipment Specifications."**

2. STRIKING CUE BALL. Legal shots require that the *cue ball* be struck only with the *cue tip*. Failure to meet this requirement is a *foul*.

3. LAG FOR BREAK. The following procedure is used for the *lag* for the *opening break*. Each player should use balls of equal size and weight (preferably cue balls but, when not available, non-striped object balls). With the balls in hand behind the *head string*, one player to the left and one to the right of the *head spot*, the balls are shot simultaneously to the *foot cushion* and back to the head end of the table. The player whose ball is the closest to the innermost edge of the head cushion wins the lag. The lagged ball must contact the foot cushion at least once. Other cushion contacts are immaterial, except as prohibited below.

It is an automatic loss of the lag if: (1) the ball crosses into the opponent's half of the table, or (2) the ball fails to contact the foot cushion, or (3) the ball drops into a pocket, or (4) the ball *jumps* the table. If both players violate automatic-loss lag rules, or if the referee is unable to determine which ball is closer, the lag is a tie and is replayed.

4. OPENING BREAK SHOT. The opening break shot is determined by either lag or *lot*. (The lag for break procedure is required for tournament and other formal competition). The player winning the lag or lot has the choice of performing the opening break shot or assigning it to the opponent.

35

The position of the cue ball on opening break is in hand behind the head string. The object balls are positioned according to specific game rules.

5. CUE BALL ON OPENING BREAK. The *opening break shot* is taken with *cue ball in hand behind the string*. The object balls are positioned according to specific game rules.

6. CUE BALL IN HAND BEHIND THE STRING. When the cue ball is *in hand behind the string*, it remains in hand (not in play) until the player drives the cue ball out of the kitchen by striking it with his cue tip, OR in the referee's judgement touches it with any part of the cue IN AN OBVIOUS ATTEMPT to perform a shot.

The cue ball may be ADJUSTED by the player's hand, cue, etc., so long as it remains in hand. Once the cue ball is in play per the above, it may not be impeded in any way by the player; to do so is to commit a foul.

7. POCKETED BALLS. A ball is considered as a pocketed ball if as a result of an otherwise legal shot, it drops off the bed of the table into the pocket and remains there. (A ball that drops out of a ball return system onto the floor is not to be construed as a ball that has not remained pocketed.) A ball that rebounds from a pocket back onto the table bed is not a pocketed ball.

8. POSITION OF BALLS. The position of a ball is judged by where it's base (or center) rests.

9. FOOT ON FLOOR. It is a foul if a player shoots when at least one foot is not in contact with the floor. Foot attire must be normal in regard to size, shape and manner in which it is worn.

10. SHOOTING WITH BALLS IN MOTION. It is a foul if a player shoots while the cue ball or any object ball is in motion (a spinning ball is in motion).

11. COMPLETION OF STROKE. A stroke is not complete (and therefore is not counted) until all balls on the table have become motionless after the stroke (a spinning ball is in motion).

12. KITCHEN DEFINED. The *head string* is not part of the *kitchen*. Thus an object that is dead center on the head string is playable when specific game rules require that a player must shoot at a ball outside of the kitchen. Likewise, the cue ball when being put in play from the kitchen (cue ball in hand behind the string), may not be placed directly on the head string; it must be behind it.

13. FOULS BY TOUCHING BALLS. It is a foul to strike, touch or in any way make contact with the cue ball in play or any object balls in play with anything (the body, clothing, chalk, mechanical bridge, cue shaft, etc.) EXCEPT the cue tip (while attached to the cue shaft), which may contact the cue ball in the execution of a legal shot.

14. FOULS BY DOUBLE HITS. It is a foul if the cue ball is struck more than once on a shot by the cue tip. (Such shots are usually referred to as *double hits*.) If, in the referee's judgement, the cue ball has left initial contact with the cue tip and then is struck a second time in the course of the same stroke, it shall be a foul.

(Note: this can be a difficult call in officiating, because on shots where the distance between the cue ball and the object ball is very short, the referee must judge whether the cue ball had time to move out of contact with the cue tip prior to being impeded and then propelled again by the follow through of the stroke. Nonetheless, if it is judged, by virtue of sound, ball position and action, and stroke used, that there were two separate contacts of the cue ball by the cue tip on a stroke, the stroke is a foul and must be so called.)

15. PUSH SHOT FOULS. It is a foul if the cue ball is pushed by the cue tip, with contact being maintained for more than the momentary time commensurate with a stroked shot. (Such shots are usually referred to as *push shots*.) If, in the referee's judgement, the player lays the cue tip against the cue ball and then pushes on into the shot, maintaining contact beyond the normal momentary split-second, the stroke is a foul and must be so called.

16. JUMPED CUE BALL. When a stroke results in the cue ball being a *jumped ball*, the stroke is a foul. (Note: jumped object balls may or may not be fouls; see specific game rules.)

17. GENERAL RULE, ALL FOULS. Though the penalties for fouls differ from game to game, the following apply to all fouls: (1) player's inning ends, and (2) if on a stroke, the stroke is invalid and any pocketed balls are not counted to the shooter's credit.

18. ILLEGAL JUMPING OF BALL. It is a foul if a player strikes the cue ball below center ("digs under" it) and intentionally causes it to rise off the bed of the table in an effort to clear an obstructing ball. Such jumping action may occasionally occur accidentally, and such "jumps" are not to be considered fouls on their face; they may still be ruled foul strokes, if for example, the ferrule or cue shaft makes contact with the cue ball in the course of the shot.

19. PLAYER RESPONSIBILITY FOULS. The player is responsible for chalk, bridges, files and any other items or equipment he brings to, uses at, or causes to approximate the table. If he drops a piece of chalk, or knocks off a mechanical bridge head, as examples, he is guilty of a foul should such an object make contact with a cue ball or object ball in play.

20. JUMPED BALLS DEFINED. Balls coming to rest other than on the bed of the table after a stroke (on the cushion top, rail surface, floor, etc.) are considered jumped balls. Balls may bounce on the cushion tops, rails or light fixtures of the table in play without being jumped balls if they return to the bed of the table under their own power and without touching anything not a part of the table equipment. The table equipment shall consist of it's light fixture, chalk not on the bed of the table, and permanent parts of the table proper. (Balls that strike or touch anything not a part of the table equipment shall be considered jumped balls even though they might return to the bed of the table after contacting the non-equipment item[s].)

All jumped object balls are spotted when all balls have stopped moving. See specific game rules to determine whether a jumped object ball is a foul.

A jumped cue ball is a foul per Rule #16; see specific game rules for putting the cue ball in play after a jumped cue ball foul.

21. SPECIAL INTENTIONAL FOUL PENALTY. The cue ball in play shall not be intentionally struck with anything other than a cue's attached tip (such as the ferrule, shaft, etc.). While such contact is automatically a foul under the provisions of Rule #13, if the referee deems the contact to be intentional, he shall warn the player once during a match that a second violation during that match will result in the loss of the match by forfeiture. If a second violation does occur, the match must be forfeited.

22. ONE FOUL LIMIT. Unless specific game rules dictate otherwise, only one foul is assessed on a player in each inning; if different penalties can apply, the most sever penalty is the factor determining which foul is assessed.

23. BALLS MOVING SPONTANEOUSLY. If a ball shifts, settles, turns or otherwise moves "by itself," the ball shall remain in the position it assumed and play continues. A hanging ball that falls into a pocket "by itself" after being motionless for 3 seconds or longer shall be replaced as closely as possible to it's position prior to falling, and play shall continue.

If an object ball drops into a pocket "by itself" as a player shoots at it, so that the cue ball passes over the spot the ball had been on, unable to hit it, the cue ball and object ball are to be replaced to their positions prior to the stroke and the player must execute the shot again. Any other object balls disturbed on the stroke are also to be replaced to their original positions for the shot to be replayed.

24. SPOTTING BALLS. When specific game rules call for spotting balls, they shall be replaced on the table on the *long string* after the stroke is complete. A single ball is placed on the foot spot; if more than one ball is to be spotted, they are placed on the long string in ascending numerical order, beginning on the foot spot and advancing toward the foot rail.

When balls on or near the foot spot or long string interfere with the spotting of balls, the balls to be spotted are placed on the long string as close as possible to the foot spot without moving the interfering balls. Spotted balls are to be *frozen* to such interfering balls, except when the cue ball is interfering; balls to be spotted against the cue ball are placed as close as possible without being frozen.

If there is insufficient room on the long string between the foot spot and the foot rail cushion for balls that must be spotted, such balls are then placed on the extension of the long string "in front" of the foot spot (between the foot spot and the *center spot*), as near as possible to the foot spot and in the same numerical order as if they were spotted "behind" the foot spot (lowest numbered ball closest to the center of the table).

(Note: there are special spotting rules in the games of "Snooker," "Cowboy Pocket Billiards" and "Bottle Pocket billiards.")

25. JAWED BALLS. If two or more balls are locked between the *jaws* or sides of the pocket, with one or more suspended in air, the referee shall inspect the balls in position and follow this procedure: he shall visually (or physically if he desires) project each ball directly downward from it's locked position; any ball that in his judgement would fall in the pocket if so moved directly downward is a pocketed ball, while any ball that would come to rest on the bed of the table is not pocketed. The balls are then placed according to the referee's assessment, and play continues according to specific game rules as if no locking or jawing of balls had occurred.

26. ADDITIONAL POCKETED BALLS. If a player completes a legal, scoring stroke on which an object ball or balls in addition to the intended, called, required or designated ball or balls also drop, such additional balls shall be counted, credited and scored in accord with the scoring rules for the particular game. (Note: the following games have rules which modify, restrict or negate Rule #26: "Bank Pool," "Cowboy Pocket Billiards," "Cribbage," "Oneball," "One Pocket," "Poker Pocket billiards," "Snooker" and "Eightball.")

27. NON-PLAYER INTERFERENCE. If the balls are moved (or a player bumped such that play is directly affected) by a non-player during match, the balls shall be replaced as near as possible to their original positions immediately prior to the incident, and play shall resume with no penalty on the player affected. If the match is officiated, the referee shall replace the balls. This rule shall also apply to "act of God" interference, such as earthquake, hurricane, light fixture falling, power failure, etc.

28. BREAKING SUBSEQUENT RACKS. When *short rack games* are being competed in a format requiring sets or races, winner of each game breaks the next. The following are common options that may be designated by tournament officials: (1) Players alternate break. (2) Loser breaks. (3) Player trailing in games score breaks the next game.

29. PLAY BY INNINGS. Unless individual game rules specify differently, players alternate turns (innings) at the table, with a player's inning ending when he either fails to legally pocket a ball, or fouls.

When an inning ends free of a foul, the incoming player accepts the table in position (unless individual game rules indicate otherwise).

30. OBJECT BALL FROZEN TO CUSHION OR CUE BALL. This rule applies to any shot where the cue ball's first contact with a ball is with one that is frozen to a cushion or to the cue ball itself. After the cue ball makes contact with the frozen object ball, the shot must result in either (1) a ball being pocketed, or (2) the cue ball contacting a cushion, or (3) the frozen ball being caused to contact a cushion (not merely rebounding from the cushion it was frozen to), or (4) another object ball being caused to contact a cushion to which it was not already in contact with. Failure to satisfy one of those four requirements is a foul. (Note: 14.1 and other games specify additional requirements and applications of this rule; see specific game rules.)

31. PLAYING FROM BEHIND THE STRING. When a player has the cue ball in hand behind the string (in the kitchen), he must drive the cue ball to a point outside the kitchen before it contacts either a cushion or an object ball. Failure to do so is either a foul, or at opponent's option, offending player can be required to replay the shot again with the balls restored to their positions prior to the shot (and with no foul penalty imposed).

Exception: if an object ball lies on or outside the head string (and is thus playable) but so close that the cue ball contacts it before the cue ball is out of the kitchen, the ball can be legally played.

POCKET BILLIARD GAMES

——— EIGHT BALL ———

Except when clearly contradicted by these additional rules,
the **General Rules of Pocket Billiards** apply.

OBJECT OF THE GAME: The game is *Call Shot* and is played with a cue ball and fifteen object balls, numbered 1 thru 15. One player must pocket balls of the group numbered 1 thru 7 (solid colors), while the other player has 9 thru 15 (stripes). THE PLAYER POCKETING HIS OR HER GROUP FIRST AND THEN LEGALLY POCKETING THE 8-BALL, WINS THE GAME.

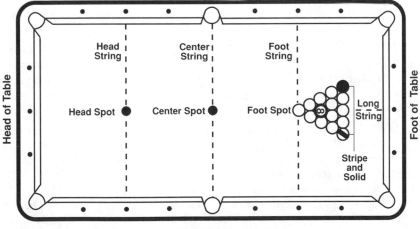

Diagram No. 1

CALL SHOT (GENTLEMEN'S CALL): In Gentlemen's Call, obvious balls and pockets do not have to be indicated. It is the opponents right to ask which ball and pocket if he is unsure of the shot. Banks and combinations are not considered obvious and both the object ball and the pocket must be called.When calling the shot, it is NEVER necessary to indicate details such as the number of *cushions, banks, kisses, caroms,* etc. If the object ball is not legally pocketed and other object balls are pocketed, then the shooter's balls that were pocketed would be

41

spotted and any of the opponent's balls remain pocketed; however if playing on a table designed for coin operation, all pocketed balls would remain pocketed. PLEASE NOTE: Any place in the rules that states to spot an illegally pocketed ball will only apply if the table is NOT designed for coin operated play.

THE RACK: The balls are *racked* in a triangle at the foot of the table with the 8-ball in the center of the triangle, the first ball of the rack on the footspot, a stripe ball in one corner of the rack and a solid ball in the other corner, as illustrated.

ALTERNATING BREAK: Winner of coin toss has option to *break*. During individual competition, players will alternate breaking on each subsequent game.

LEGAL BREAK SHOT: (Defined) To execute a legal break, the breaker (with the cue ball behind the headstring) must either (1) pocket a ball, or (2) drive four numbered balls to the rail. If he fails to make a legal break, it is *not* a foul, however, the incoming player has the option of (1) accepting the table in position and shooting, or (2) having the balls re-racked and shooting the opening break himself. It is *not* necessary to hit the head ball (the ball that is on the foot spot) to initiate a legal break in 8-ball.

SCRATCH ON A LEGAL BREAK: If a player *scratches* on a legal break shot, (1) all balls pocketed remain pocketed except the 8-ball which is spotted, (2) it is a foul, (3) the table is open. PLEASE NOTE: Incoming player has *cue ball* in hand behind the *headstring* and may not shoot an object ball that is behind the headstring, unless he first shoots the cue ball past the headstring and then by hitting a rail causing the cue ball to come back behind the headstring and hit the object ball.

8-BALL POCKETED ON THE BREAK: If the 8-ball is pocketed on the break, the breaker may ask for a re-rack or have the 8-ball spotted and continue shooting. If the breaker scratches while pocketing the 8-ball on the break, the incoming player has the option of a re-rack or having the 8-ball spotted and begin shooting with ball in hand behind the headstring.

HEADSTRING RULE: This rule applies only when the opening player scratches on the break, and the incoming player has ball in hand behind the headstring. The incoming player may place the cue ball anywhere on or behind the headstring. If the player places the cue ball in front of the headstring and shoots, it is a foul. He may shoot at any object ball as long as the base of the object ball is past the headstring. He may not shoot at any ball that the base of the ball is on or behind the headstring, unless he first shoots the cue ball past the headstring and then by hitting a rail causing the cue ball to come back behind the headstring and hit the object ball. The base of the ball (the point of the ball touching the table) determines whether it is within or out of the headstring. If the incoming player inadvertently places the cue ball in front of the headstring, it is a good gesture for his opponent to inform him before he shoots to avoid confusion.

OPEN TABLE: (Defined) The table is "open" when the choice of groups (stripes or solids) has not yet been determined. When the table is open, it is legal to hit a solid first to make a stripe or vice-versa. Note: The table is always open immediately after the break shot. When the table is open it is legal to hit a solid or the 8-ball first to make a called stripe or vice-versa. On an open table, all illegally pocketed balls are spotted.

CHOICE OF GROUP: The choice of stripes or solids is not determined on the break even if balls are made from only one or both groups. THE TABLE IS ALWAYS OPEN IMMEDIATELY AFTER THE BREAK SHOT. The choice of group is only determined when a player legally pockets a called object ball after the break shot.

LEGAL SHOT: (Defined) On all shots (except on the break and when the table is *open*), the shooter must hit one of his group of balls first and, (1) pocket an object ball, or (2) cause the cue ball or any object ball to contact a *rail*. PLEASE NOTE: It is okay for the shooter to bank the cue ball off a rail before contacting his object ball, however, after contact with his object ball, an object ball must be pocketed, OR the cue ball or any object ball must contact a rail.

SAFETY PLAY: Safety play is defined as a legal shot. If the shooting player intends to play safe by pocketing an obvious object ball, then prior to the shot, he must declare a safety to his opponent. If this is NOT done, the shooter will be required to shoot again. The shooter's object ball is considered illegally pocketed and must be spotted.

SCORING: A player is entitled to continue shooting until he fails to legally pocket a ball of his group. After a player has legally pocketed all of his group of balls, he shoots to pocket the 8-ball.

FOULS: The following infractions result in fouls:

1. Failure to execute a legal shot as defined above.
2. A scratch shot (shooting the cue ball into a pocket or off the table).
3. A scratch shot on a legal break.
4. Shooting without at least one foot touching the floor.
5. Moving or touching the cue ball in any fashion by means other than legal play is a foul.
6. Shooting a jump shot over another ball by scooping the cue stick under the cue ball is illegal and a foul. A jump shot executed by striking the cue ball above center is legal. PLEASE NOTE: A player does not commit a foul when he accidentally *miscues* and causes the cue ball to jump above the surface of the table.
7. In organized competition (league or tournament play) if a team member advises or coaches another team member who is the shooter at the time, it is a foul on the team member shooting.

FOUL PENALTY: Opposing player gets *cue ball in hand*. This means that the player can place the cue ball anywhere on the table (does not have to be behind the headstring except on opening break). This rule prevents a player from making intentional fouls which would put his opponent at a disadvantage. With "cue ball in hand," the player may position the cue ball on the table by hand (more than once if necessary). After placing the cue ball, the shaft and *ferrule* of the cue stick (not the tip) may also be used for positioning the cue ball for shooting.

COMBINATION SHOTS: Combination shots are allowed: however, the 8-ball cannot be used as a first ball in the combination except when the table is open.

ILLEGALLY POCKETED BALLS: An object ball is considered to be illegally pocketed when (1) that object ball is pocketed on the same shot a foul is committed, or (2) the called ball did not go in the designated pocket, or (3) a safety is called prior to the shot. If not on tables designed for coin-operated play, the shooter's illegally pocketed balls are spotted on the foot spot and opponent's balls remain pocketed. If playing on tables designed for coin-operated play, all illegally pocketed balls remain off the table.

SPOTTING BALLS: Whenever an object ball is to be spotted, the object ball is spotted on the *long string* as close to the *foot spot* as possible and shall be *frozen* to any interfering ball except the cue ball.

Spotting Balls

11 Balls on and Behind Spot

Long String

Foot String

Foot Spot

Diagram No. 2

OBJECT BALLS JUMPED OFF THE TABLE: If any object ball is jumped off the table, it is a miss and loss of turn, not a foul, unless it is the 8-ball, which is a loss of game. The shooter's object ball(s) is spotted and any of the opponent's jumped balls will be pocketed.

OBJECT BALL FROZEN TO CUSHION: This rule applies when the object ball to be struck by the cue ball is frozen to the rail. After the cue ball contacts the object ball you must (1) pocket the frozen ball or any other object ball, or (2) drive the frozen object ball to another cushion, or (3) drive the cue ball or another object ball to any cushion. Failure to do so is a foul. When there is any doubt whether the object ball is frozen to a cushion, the player should for a ruling before shooting.

PUSH SHOT: If the cue ball is touching your object ball prior to the shot, the player may shoot towards it with a level cue, providing that his cue stick strikes rather than pushes the cue ball. If the cue ball is close, but not frozen to the object ball, the cue must be elevated to a 45 degree angle when shooting in the general direction of the line of the two balls. A level cue may be used if aiming 45 degrees or more off the line of the two balls.

LOSS OF GAME: A player loses the game if he commits any of the following infractions:

1. Fouls when pocketing the 8-ball.
2. Pockets the 8-ball on the same stroke as the last of his group of balls.
3. Jumps the 8-ball off the table at any time.
4. Pockets the 8-ball in a pocket other than the one designated.
5. Pockets the 8-ball when it is not the legal object ball.

NOTE: When shooting at the 8-ball, a scratch or foul is not loss of game if the 8-ball is not pocketed or jumped from the table.

STALEMATED GAME: If in 3 consecutive turns at the table by each player (6 turns total), they purposely foul or scratch and both players agree that attempting to pocket or move an object ball will result in immediate loss of game, then the game will be considered a stalemate. The balls will then be re-racked and the breaker of the stalemated game will break again. PLEASE NOTE: Three consecutive fouls by one player is not a loss of game.

DISQUALIFICATION: The League or Tournament Director has the right to disqualify any player from competition and the player forfeits the right to prize money and/or any other awards for unsportsmanlike conduct or tactics detrimental to the league or tournament.

SPECTATOR COACHING: Spectators on the sidelines should not be allowed to advise or coach a player during competition. If after asking a spectator not to coach a player and he continues to do so, the Referee should ask the spectator to leave the tournament area.

SHOOTING TIME RULE: If in the opinion of the Referee a player is impeding the progress of the Tournament or game with consistently slow play, the Referee can warn the player and then at his discretion impose a one minute time limit for that person between shots. If the Referee does impose a one minute time limit and that limit is exceeded, a foul will be called and the incoming player shall have ball in hand.

NINE BALL

Except when clearly contradicted by these additional rules,
the **General Rules of Pocket Billiards** apply.

OBJECT OF THE GAME: The object of the game is to pocket the 9-ball. Pocketing the 9-ball either on the break or any other legal shot, wins the game.

TYPE OF GAME: Nine Ball is a variation of *call shot* rotation in which the lowest numbered ball on the table must be the player's first *cue ball* contact. If a player complies, any called pocketed ball counts. For example, if a player strikes the one ball legally and the *caroms* or by *combination* pockets the nine ball which he has called in the pocket he has designated, that player wins the game. Nine Ball is probably today's most popular action-oriented game, since it is fast, easy for spectators to follow and results in spectacular shot-making; a fast and exciting game.

When calling the shot it is never necessary to indicate details such as; cushions, banks, kisses, caroms, etc.

CALL SHOT: When a ball is pocketed in a designated pocket, additional balls pocketed during the same shot will count. When no ball is called or a *safety* is called and a ball is pocketed, or if called ball falls in wrong pocket, the incoming player has the option of shooting or forcing his opponent to shoot again. When calling the shot it is never necessary to indicate details such as; *cushions, banks, kisses, caroms,* etc. Unless obvious to both referee and/or opponent, the shooter must either declare a called shot, safety, or push. Any bank shot is never obvious and must be called.

PLAYERS: 2 or more.

BALLS USED: Object balls 1-9, plus *cue ball.*

THE RACK: "Diamond" *rack* (rows 1-2-3-2-1) with the 1 ball on the foot spot, and the 9 ball in the diamond's center; other balls may be placed entirely at random. (See Diagram 3)

Diagram No. 3
Diamond Shaped Rack
1-Ball must be on the foot spot.
9-Ball must be in the center of the rack.

OPENING BREAK: The starting player must, (1) Strike the one ball first, (2) Drive a minimum of four *object balls* to a *rail* or pocket any object ball. If starting player fails to do any of the above, the incoming player has *cue ball in hand* anywhere on the table. Nine Ball on *break* wins. Each rack of 9-Ball will begin when the cue ball passes the *headstring* after being struck by the *cue tip.*

Calling the shot is not required on the break. Any object ball pocketed on the break counts and the player continues shooting, if he did not commit a *foul* or *scratch.*

If a player misses rack entirely, it is a foul. Cue ball is placed behind headstring & incoming player has choice of breaking or making the same player break again.

PLAY BEGINS: Each rack of 9-ball will begin when the cue ball passes the headstring after being struck by cue tip.

RULES OF PLAY:

1. A legal shot requires that the cue ball's first contact be with the lowest numbered ball on the table. A player must then (1) pocket a ball where called, or (2) cause the cue ball or any object ball to contact a cushion. Failure to meet this requirement is a foul.

2. A legally pocketed ball entitles a shooter to remain at the table until he fails to pocket a ball on a legal shot.

3. When a player legally pockets a ball, he must shoot again.

4. When the 9-ball is pocketed on any legal shot, it is a win; game is over.

5. It is a loss of game if a player commits three *successive fouls.*

ILLEGALLY POCKETED BALLS: All stay pocketed (except 9-ball), no penalty.

JUMPED OBJECT BALLS: All stay pocketed; no penalty (except 9-ball).

CUE BALL AFTER JUMP OR SCRATCH: Incoming player has *cue ball in hand*, anywhere on table.

PENALTY FOR FOULS: The incoming player is awarded *cue ball in hand*, anywhere on table.

DECLARATION OF SHOT: Unless obvious to both referee and/or opponent, the shooter must either declare a called shot, safety, or push. Any *bank shot–* is never obvious an must be called.

SHOOT OUT OR PUSH AFTER BREAK: The player at the table immediately after the break has the option to Push Out or Shoot Out. A Push or Shoot Out means "intentionally committing an illegal shot to move the cue ball to better position on the required object ball." After a push, the incoming player has the option of shooting or forcing his opponent to shoot again. A push is not considered a foul. After a scratch on the break the incoming player cannot push.

BALL IN HAND: After any scratch or foul, the incoming player will have the cue ball in hand anywhere on the table. This includes after a scratch on the break except if the cue ball fails to strike any ball on opening break (see opening break).

NO BALLS SPOTTED: All illegally pocketed balls, balls pocketed during a safety or push, or *jumped object balls* will not be *spotted*. Essentially, the 9-ball is the only ball that can be spotted.

FOUL ON CUE/OBJECT BALLS: Foul on cue balls only except during tournament finals or televised matches at which time foul on all balls will apply.

WINNER BREAKS: The winner of a game shall break in the next game until a match is completed.

JUMPED BALLS: When an object ball is jumped off the table and the called ball is pocketed, there is no foul and shooting player continues.

When an object ball is jumped off the table and there is no called ball made, the incoming player has the option of shooting or having his opponent shoot again.

Nine ball on break wins.

— NINE BALL —
(PROFESSIONAL RULES)

1. SUMMARY

Nine Ball is played with nine object balls numbered one through nine and a cue ball. On each shot the first ball the cue ball contacts must be the lowest numbered ball on the table, but the balls need not be pocketed in order. If a player pockets any ball on a legal shot, he remains at the table for another shot, and continues until he misses, fouls, or wins the game by pocketing the nine ball. After a miss, the incoming player must shoot from the position left by the previous player, but after a foul the incoming player may start with the cue ball anywhere on the table. Certain *serious fouls* are penalized by loss of the game. Players are not required to call any shot. A match ends when one of the players has won the required number of games.

Detailed rules for nine ball are given below, followed by the definitions of some technical terms. These rules do not cover specifications of tables and balls, sanctioning conditions, or the handling of prize funds.

2. BEGINNING PLAY

2.1 Order of Play

Order of play for the first game is determined by lag. The winner of the lag may break the first rack or assign the break to his opponent. In subsequent games of the match the winner of the previous game will break.

2.2 Racking the Balls

The object balls are racked in a diamond shape, with the one ball at the top of the diamond and on the foot spot, the nine ball in the center of the diamond, and the other balls in arbitrary order. If the one ball is not touching both of the adjacent balls, the breaker may ask the referee to rerack the balls prior to the break. The cue ball begins in hand above the head string.

2.3 Break Shot

The rules governing the break shot are the same as for other shots except:

a. If the cue ball is pocketed or driven off the table, and no other foul is committed, the incoming player has cue ball in hand above the head string. If the one ball is not below the head string, it is spotted on the long string. The incoming player may pass the shot after a scratch on the break, and the breaker must then shoot with ball in hand above the head string.

b. The breaker must attempt an "open break" – he must attempt to pocket a ball. Failure to do so is a standard foul.

c. If the breaker fails to contact the one ball, it is not considered a foul, the balls are reracked (if necessary), and the breaker breaks again, starting from behind the head string.

d. On the shot immediately following a legal break, the shooter may play a "push out." (See Section 9.11.)

3. CONTINUING PLAY

If the breaker pockets one or more balls on a legal break, he continues to shoot until he misses, fouls, or wins the game. If the player misses or fouls, the other player begins his inning and shoots until he misses, fouls, or wins. The game ends when the nine ball is pocketed on a legal shot, or the game is forfeited for a serious infraction of the rules.

4. STANDARD FOULS

When a player commits a *standard foul*, he must relinquish his run at the table and all balls pocketed on the foul shot are spotted on the long string in numerical order. The incoming player is awarded ball in hand; prior to his first shot he may place the cue ball anywhere on the table. If a player fouls during the other player's inning, the shooter is awarded ball in hand, and if the foul had an effect on the position of the balls, the referee will restore the position if requested to do so by the shooter. If a player commits several *standard fouls* on one shot, they are counted as only one foul. The following are *standard fouls*:

4.1. Scratch

Pocketing the cue ball or driving it off the table is a foul.

4.2. Bad Hit

If the first object ball contacted by the cue ball is not the lowest numbered ball on the table, the shot is foul.

4.3. No rail

If no object ball is pocketed, failure to drive the cue ball or some object ball to a rail after the cue ball contacts the object ball is a foul.

4.4. Foot

Failure to have at least one foot in contact with the floor at the moment the cue tip contacts the cue ball is a foul.

4.5. Moving Ball

Shooting while any ball is moving or spinning is a foul.

4.6. Push Shot or Double Stroke

If the cue ball is touching the lowest numbered ball prior to the shot, the player may shoot towards it, providing that his cue stick strikes rather than pushes the cue ball. (the PBA has not yet adopted a rule covering the situation when the cue ball is close to but not touching the object ball.)

4.7. Touched Object Ball

It is a foul to touch a moving ball or to allow that ball to hit any foreign object, such as a cube of chalk. (The top of the rail is not considered to be a foreign object.) It is not a foul to accidentally touch stationary object balls while in the act of shooting. If such an accident occurs, the player should allow the referee to restore the object balls to their correct positions. If the player does not allow such a restoration, and a ball set in motion as a normal part of the shot touches such an unrestored ball, or passes partly into a region originally occupied by a disturbed ball, the shot is foul. In short, if the accident has any effect on the outcome of the shot it is a foul. In any case, the referee must restore the positions of the disturbed balls as soon as possible, but not during the shot. It is a foul to play another shot before the referee has restored any accidentally moved balls.

At the nonshooting player's option, the disturbed balls will be left in their new positions. In this case, the balls are considered restored, and subsequent contact on them is not a foul.

If the match is to be televised, touching a stationary ball is a foul. The incoming player still has the option of restoration.

4.8. Placement
Touching any object ball with the cue ball while it is in hand is a foul.

4.9. Object Ball
Players may touch object balls only to assist the referee in his duties. If a player intentionally touches any object ball for any other purpose while a game is in progress, whether that object ball is in play or not, he has fouled. (This rule does not apply to the usual collisions between the balls.)

4.10. Cue Ball
Except for ball in hand placement, if a player touches the cue ball with anything other than the chalked surface of his cue tip, he has fouled. The player may place the cue ball with anything other than the chalked surface of his cue tip.

4.11. Scoop Shot
If a player plays a shot with extreme draw with the intention of miscuing to make the cue ball jump over some obstruction, he has fouled. (See Jump Shots, section 6.3) Any miscue when executing a jump shot is a foul.

4.12. Interference
If the nonshooting player distracts his opponent or interferes with his play, he has fouled. If a player shoots out of turn, or moves any ball except during his inning, it is considered to be interference.

4.13. Devices
Using any device in an uncustomary manner in lining up or executing a shot is a foul.

4.14. Practice
While a game is in progress, practice is not allowed. Taking a shot that is not part of that game is a foul.

5. SERIOUS FOULS
The following *serious fouls* are penalized by the loss of one game, if the referee has warned the player before the foul. If the referee fails to warn the player, any foul is penalized like a *standard foul*, except as noted.

5.1. Three Consecutive Fouls
If a player fouls three times without making an intervening legal shot, he loses the game. The three fouls must occur in one game. The warning must be given between the second and third fouls.

5.2. Assistance
While a match is in progress, players are not allowed to ask spectators for assistance in planning or executing shots. If a player asks for and receives such assistance, he loses the game. Any spectator who spontaneously offers any significant help to a player will be removed from the area. (See section 7.10)

5.3. Failure to Leave the Table

If a player does not stop shooting as soon as the referee has called a foul, he loses the game. The calling of the foul is considered to be the referee's warning to the player.

5.4. Slow Play

If the referee feels a player is playing exceptionally slowly, he must warn the player that he risks loss of a game if such slow play continues. Subsequently, if the referee and the tournament director agree that his play remains unacceptably slow, they may penalize the player one game for each game in which such slow play continues. (In general, no shot should take more than two minutes to plan and execute.)

5.5. Head String

After a scratch on a break shot, the cue ball is in hand above the head string. The referee should say, "Above the head string," when he hands the cue ball to the player, which constitutes the warning. If the player intentionally places the cue ball below the head string he loses the game. If the player accidentally places the cue ball slightly below the head string, the referee must warn him again, or no foul is considered to have occurred. With cue ball in hand above the head string, if the player plays directly on an object ball above the head string without the cue ball first crossing the head string, he loses the game. No warning is required in this last case.

5.6. Suspended Play

If a player shoots while play is suspended by the referee, he loses the game. Announcement of the suspension is considered sufficient warning.

5.7. Concession

If a player concedes, he loses the game. The unscrewing of a jointed cue stick, except to replace a shaft, is considered to be a concession. No warning from the referee is required in the case of a concession.

6. OTHER SITUATIONS AND INTERPRETATIONS

6.1. Outside Interference

When outside interference occurs during a shot that has an effect on the outcome of that shot, the referee will restore the balls to the positions they had before the shot, and the shot will be replayed. If the interference had no effect on the shot, the referee will restore the disturbed balls and play will continue.

6.2. Settling into place

A ball may settle slightly after it appears to have stopped, possibly due to slight imperfections in the ball or the table. Unless this causes a ball to fall into a pocket, it is considered a normal hazard of play, and the ball will not be moved back. If a ball falls into a pocket as the result of such settling, it is replaced as close as possible to its original position. If a ball falls into a pocket during or just prior to a shot, and has an effect on the shot, the referee will restore the position and the shot will be replayed. Players are not penalized for shooting while a ball is settling.

6.3. Jump Shots

It is legal to cause the cue ball to rise off the bed of the table by elevating the cue stick on the shot, and forcing the cue ball to rebound from the bed of the table. (See section 4.11.)

6.4. Protesting Fouls

If a player thinks that the referee has failed to call a foul, he must protest to the referee before the next shot starts. If he fails to do so, and the foul goes unpenalized, the foul is considered not to have occurred. The referee is the final judge on matters of fact. If either player thinks that the referee is applying the rules incorrectly, and the dispute cannot be resolved by reference to the rules, the referee must take the protest to the tournament director or his appointed substitute. The tournament director's decision on interpretation of the rules is final. A player may also protest if he thinks that the referee has called a foul incorrectly. In any case play is suspended until the protest is resolved.

6.5. Prompting Warnings

When a player thinks that the referee is failing to issue a mandatory warning, he may remind the referee that such a warning is necessary.

6.6. Waiving Specific Rules

Prior to the start of the tournament, the tournament director may choose to waive or modify specific rules, e.g. the loser of a game rather than the winner may break the following games.

6.7. Late Start

A player must be ready to begin a match within fifteen minutes of the start of the match, or his opponent wins by forfeit. The starting time is considered to be the scheduled time or the time the match is announced, whichever is later.

6.8. Unsportsmanlike Conduct

If the referee and the tournament director agree that a player is persistently behaving in a disruptive or unsportsmanlike manner, they may penalize him in any way they choose, including calling a foul on him, awarding the game or match to his opponent, or forfeiting all of his remaining matches.

7. INSTRUCTIONS FOR THE REFEREE

The referee will maintain order and enforce these rules. He is the final judge in all matters of fact. His duties include but are not limited to the following:

7.1. Before the Match

Before the match, the referee will clean the table and balls if necessary. He will ensure that chalk and mechanical bridges are available. He will mark the head string and long string with a pencil, if they are not already marked.

7.2. Racking

The referee will rack the balls as tightly as possible, which means each ball should be touching its neighbors. Tapping a ball into place is not recommended; it is preferable to thoroughly brush the area of the rack to even out the cloth.

7.3. Calling Fouls

The referee will call fouls as soon as they occur and will inform the incoming player that he has ball in hand.

7.4. Clearing Pockets

On tables which do not have ball return systems, the referee will remove pocketed object balls from full or nearly full pockets. It is the player's responsibility to see that this duty is performed; he has no recourse if a ball rebounds from a full pocket.

7.5. Cleaning Balls

During a game a player may ask the referee to clean one or more balls. The referee will clean any visibly soiled ball.

7.6. Soliciting Information

If the referee does not have a clear view of a possible foul, he may ask spectators for assistance in determining what occurred. The referee will then weigh all evidence as he sees fit.

7.7. Warnings Which Are Mandatory

The referee must warn a player who is about to commit a serious foul, otherwise any foul is considered to be a standard foul (except as specially noted). The referee must warn a player who has had two consecutive fouls, otherwise the player is considered to have had only one foul prior to the shot. The referee must warn a player when an object ball is touching a rail, otherwise any contact on that ball is considered to have driven it to that rail. The referee should issue warnings as soon as the corresponding situation arises. A warning given just as a shot starts is not considered sufficient; the player must be given enough time to react.

7.8. Restoring a Position

When it becomes necessary, the referee will restore disturbed balls to their original positions to the best of his ability. The referee may ask for information for this purpose if he is not sure of the original position.

If the balls were disturbed by a player, the other player has the option of preventing the restoration. In this case, the referee should clearly indicate where the balls will be moved to if they are restored, and only restore the balls if requested to do so.

7.9. Advice and Rules Clarifications

The referee must not give advice to the players on points of play except to clarify the rules. When asked for such clarification, the referee will explain the applicable rules to the best of his ability, but any misstatement by the referee will not protect a player from enforcement of the actual rules. When asked, the referee must tell a player how many consecutive fouls have been committed, what the score is, whether the cue ball is touching an object ball, what the restored position would be, etc.

7.10. Suspending Play

The referee has the authority to suspend play during protests by players and whenever he feels that conditions are unsuitable for play to continue. If a spectator is interfering with the game, play may be suspended until that spectator is removed from the area.

8. PLAYING WITHOUT A REFEREE

When a referee is not available, the player who is not shooting will assume the duties of the referee.

8.1. Third Opinion

When a shot comes up that seems likely to lead to controversy, a third person should be temporarily enlisted to provide a third opinion.

8.2. Resolving Disputes

Any dispute between the two players will be resolved by the tournament director or his appointed substitute.

9. DEFINITIONS

The following definitions apply throughout these rules.

9.1. Shot, Inning, Game, Match

A shot begins at the instant the cue tip contacts the cue ball, and ends when all balls in play stop rolling and spinning. (See section 9.3)

A player's inning begins when it is legal for him to take a shot and ends at the end of a shot on which he misses, fouls or wins, or when he fouls between shots.

A game starts when the referee has finished racking the balls, and ends at the end of a legal shot which pockets the nine or when a player forfeits the game as the result of a foul.

A match starts when the players are ready to lag and ends when the deciding game ends.

9.2. Above the Head String

A ball is above the head string if its center is above the head string (toward the head end of the table). A ball is below the head string if its center is below the head string (toward the foot or rack-end of the table).

9.3. Stopped

A ball resting on the brink of a pocket is considered to have stopped if it remains motionless for five seconds, as determined by the referee. If any player or spectator causes such a ball to fall in before the five second limit by bumping or otherwise moving the table, the ball will be replaced at the edge of the pocket and is not considered pocketed. The time begins when all other balls have stopped and the shot ends at the end of the five seconds.

9.4. Pocketed

A ball is considered pocketed when it comes to rest in a pocket or enters the ball return system of the table. A ball which hits the lining of the pocket or another ball already in the pocket and returns to the surface of the table or jumps off the table, is not considered pocketed. If a ball comes to rest at the brink of a pocket so that it is partly supported by another ball, it is considered to be pocketed if the removal of the supporting ball would cause the supported ball to fall into the pocket.

9.5. To a Rail

A ball is driven to a rail if it is not touching a rail, and then touches a rail. A ball which is touching a rail at the start of a shot and then is forced into the same rail is not considered to have been driven to that rail unless it leaves the rail and returns. A ball is considered to have been driven to a rail if it is driven off the table or touches the pocket back or facing.

9.6. Spotting Balls

All object balls that have been pocketed illegally or driven off the table are spotted by the referee after the shot is over. Object balls are spotted by placing them on the long string, on or below the foot spot if possible, and as close to the foot spot as possible. If several balls are to be spotted at the same time, they are spotted in numerical order.

9.7. In Hand
When the cue ball is in hand, the player may place the cue ball anywhere on the bed of the table, except in contact with an object ball. He may continue to adjust the position of the cue ball until he takes a shot. With ball in hand above the head string, (after a scratch on the break), the player may not place the cue ball below the head string.

9.8. Off the Table
An unpocketed ball is considered to be driven off the table if it comes to rest other than on the bed of the table. It is not a foul to drive an object ball off the table. It is spotted and play continues.

9.9. Miscue
A miscue occurs when the tip of the cue stick slides off the cue ball due to insufficient chalk or to a contact point too far from center. It is usually accompanied by a sharp sound and a departure of the cue ball from its expected line of travel.

9.10. Lag
Players lag by shooting at the same time from behind the head string to contact the foot rail and then have the cue ball come to rest as close as possible to the head rail. Object balls may be substituted if two cue balls are not available. A player loses the lag if his cue ball crosses the centerline of the table, does not contact the foot rail, is pocketed or driven off the table, or hits any object ball. Ties are replayed. The distance of the cue ball to the head rail is the shortest distance between the cue ball and any cloth-covered part of the rail (the cushion nose or the pocket facing).

9.11. Push Out
The player who shoots the shot immediately after a legal break may play a push out. On a push out, the cue ball is not required to contact any object ball nor any rail, so Rules 4.2 and 4.3 are suspended, but all other foul rules still apply. The player must announce his intention of playing a push out before the shot, or the shot is considered to be a normal shot. Any ball pocketed on a push out does not count and is spotted. Following a legal push out, the incoming player is permitted to shoot from that position or to pass the shot back to the player who pushed out. A push out is not considered to be a foul as long as no rule (except 4.2 or 4.3) is violated. An illegal push out is penalized according to the type of foul committed.

Rules provided by the Men's Professional Billiard Association, 3785 Hwy. 167, Richfield, WI 53076

14.1 CONTINUOUS

Except when clearly contradicted by these additional rules,
the **General Rules of Pocket Billiards** apply.

TYPE OF GAME: 14.1 Continuous is generally considered to be the game that provides the greatest all-around test of complete pocket billiard playing skill, requiring great concentration, accuracy, shot-making, defense, patience and knowledge. It is the only commonly played game in which a shooter can play a single inning through rack after rack of balls. Players may shoot at any ball on the table at any time, but they must call the ball and the pocket on each shot. Unending variety... and challenge!

PLAYERS: 2 (or 2 teams).

BALLS USED: Standard set of object balls numbered 1-15, plus *cue ball*.

THE RACK: Standard *triangle* rack with the front apex ball on the *foot spot*, 1 ball on the racker's right corner, 5 ball on left corner. Other balls placed at random.

OBJECT OF THE GAME: Score the pre-determined point total for a game prior to the opponent (usually 150 in major tournament play or any agreed upon total in casual play.)

SCORING: Any ball legally pocketed counts one point for the shooter.

OPENING BREAK: Starting player must either (1) designate a ball and a pocket into which that ball will be pocketed and accomplish the shot, or (2) cause the cue ball to contact a ball and then a cushion, plus cause two object balls to contact a cushion. Failure to meet at least one of the above requirements is a *breaking violation*. Offender's score is assessed a two point penalty for each breaking violation. In addition, the opponent has the choice of (1) accepting the *table in position*, or (2) having the balls reracked and requiring the offending player to repeat the opening break. That choice continues until the opening break is not a breaking violation, or until the opponent accepts the table in position. The three *successive fouls* rule does not apply to breaking violations.

   If the starting player scratches on a legal opening break, he is charged with a foul and assessed a one point penalty, which applies toward the "Successive Fouls Penalties." The incoming player is awarded *cue ball in hand behind the head string*, with object balls in position.

RULES OF PLAY:

   1. A legally pocketed ball entitles a shooter to continue at the table until he fails to legally pocket a *called ball* on a shot. A player may shoot any ball he chooses, but before he shoots, must designate the called ball and *called pocket*. He need not indicate any detail such as *kisses, caroms, combinations,* or *cushions* (all of which are legal). Any additionally pocketed ball(s) on a legal stroke is scored as one point for the shooter.

   If a referee incorrectly calls a shot, a player should correct him before completing the shot. If a mis-call does occur for any reason, the shot shall be credited if, in the referee's judgement, the player did legally execute the shot as intended.

2. On all shots, a player must cause the cue ball to contact an object ball and then (1) pocket an object ball, or (2) cause the cue ball or any object ball to contact a cushion. Failure to meet these requirements is a foul.

When a object ball is not *frozen* to a cushion, but is within a ball's width of a cushion (referee to determine by measurement if necessary), a player is permitted only two legal safeties on that ball using only the near rail. If such safety play is employed that object ball is then considered frozen to the rail on the players next inning. The **General Rules of Pocket Billiards**, "Frozen Balls" requirements apply if the player chooses to make his first cue ball contact with that object ball on his third shot.

(**Note:** If a player has committed a foul on his previous shot effort before playing this ball, he is allowed only one legal safety on the ball using the near rail. He must then meet the requirements of the "Frozen Ball" rule on his next shot. If he has committed two consecutive fouls, he must immediately meet the requirements of the "Frozen Ball" rule when playing this object ball. If such player fails to meet the requirements of the "Frozen Ball" rule, he is considered to have committed a third successive foul and the appropriate point penalty is assessed as well as one point for each of the previous fouls. All fifteen balls are then reracked and the player committing the infraction is required to break as at the beginning of the game.)

3. When the fourteenth ball of a rack is pocketed, play stops momentarily with the fifteenth ball remaining in position on the table; the fourteen pocketed balls are then racked (with the space at the foot spot vacant in the triangle). Player then continues, normally pocketing the fifteenth (or "break" ball) in such manner as to have the cue ball carom into the rack and spread the balls to facilitate the continuance of his run. However, player is not compelled to shoot the fifteenth ball; he may shoot any ball he desires.

See Diagram #6 if the fifteenth ball is pocketed on the same stroke as the fourteenth ball.

4. A player may call a *safety* rather than an object ball (for defensive purposes). Safety play is legal, but must comply with all applicable rules. Player's inning ends when a safety is played, and pocketed balls are not scored. Any object ball pocketed on a called safety is spotted.

5. A player may not catch, touch, or in any way interfere with a ball as it travels toward a pocket or the rack area on a shot (to include catching a ball as it enters a pocket by having a hand in the pocket). If he does, he is charged with a special "deliberate foul" and is penalized one point for the foul and an additional fifteen point penalty, for a total of sixteen points. The incoming player then has choice of (1) accepting the *table in position* with the cue ball in hand behind the head string, or (2) having all fifteen balls reracked and requiring the offending player to shoot under the requirements of the opening break.

6. If the fifteenth (unpocketed) ball of a rack and/or the cue ball interferes with the triangle being lowered straight down into position for racking, refer to

Diagram #6, which indicates the proper manner of relocating balls. (The lined out boxes are those situations in which there is no interference, both balls remain in position.)

14.1– What to do if:

15th Ball Lies \ Cue Ball Lies	IN THE RACK	NOT IN THE RACK AND NOT ON HEAD SPOT*	ON HEAD SPOT*
IN THE RACK	15th Ball: foot spot. Cue Ball: in kitchen	15th Ball: head spot. Cue Ball: in position	15th Ball: center spot. Cue Ball: in position.
POCKETED	15th Ball: foot spot. Cue Ball: in kitchen.	15th Ball: foot spot. Cue Ball: in position	15th Ball: foot spot. Cue Ball: in position.
IN KITCHEN BUT NO ON HEAD SPOT*	15th Ball: in position. Cue Ball: head spot.		
NOT IN KITCHEN & NOT IN THE RACK	15th Ball: in position. Cue Ball: in kitchen.		
ON HEAD SPOT*	15th Ball: in position. Cue Ball: center spot.		*On head spot means to interfere with spotting a ball on the head spot

Diagram No. 6

7. When a player has the cue ball in hand behind the head string (as after a scratch) and all object balls are behind the head string, the object ball nearest the head string may be spotted at his request. If two or more balls are an equal distance from the head string, the player may designate which of the equidistant balls he desires to have spotted.

ILLEGALLY POCKETED BALLS: All spotted. No penalty.

JUMPED OBJECT BALLS: All spotted after the balls come to rest. No penalty.

CUE BALL AFTER JUMP OR SCRATCH: Incoming player has cue ball in hand behind the head string, unless the provision of Rule of Play Number 2, 5 or the "Successive Fouls Penalties" (below) apply to the offender's foul and dictate alternate choices or procedures.

PENALTIES FOR FOULS: One point deducted for each foul; NOTE: more sever penalties for deliberate fouls (rule of Play #5) and third "Successive Fouls" (below). Incoming player accepts cue ball in position unless foul was a jumped cue ball, pocket scratch, deliberate foul (Rule of Play #5) or third successive foul.

SUCCESSIVE FOUL PENALTIES: When a player commits a foul, he is penalized one point (or more as appropriate) and a notation is made and posted by the scorer that he is "on a foul." The player remains "on a foul" until his next shot attempt, at which time he may remove the foul by successfully pocketing a called ball, or completing a legal safety. If he fails to meet these requirements on his next turn at the table, he's penalized one point. The notation is changed to "on two fouls." If he fails to meet the requirements of successfully pocketing a called ball or completing a legal safety on his third consecutive turn at the table, a penalty of 20% of game total is assessed. For example: 100 point game, 20 balls; 150 point game, 30 balls.

The commission of a third successive foul automatically clears the offender's record of fouls.

All balls are then reracked and the player committing the infraction is required to break as at the beginning of the game. Rules for the opening break apply.

It should be emphasized that successive fouls must be committed in successive turns (or playing attempts), **not** merely in successive innings. For example, if a player ends inning #6 with a foul, steps to the table for inning #7 and fouls (he is "on two fouls"), and then starts inning #8 with a legally pocketed ball before scratching on his second shot attempt of the inning, he has not committed three successive fouls, even though there were fouls in three successive innings. As soon as he legally pocketed the ball to start inning #8, he cleared the two fouls. He is, of course, "on one foul" when he plays the first stroke attempt of inning #9. OPTION: At the choice of the non-offending player, the penalty for a third successive foul can be as follows: One point is deducted from the offender's score, and the cue ball is in hand for the non-offender with the object balls in position. The offender's record is cleared of successive fouls as in the standard rules.

SCORING NOTE: The deduction of penalty points can result in negative scores. A running score can read "minus one," "minus two," "minus fifteen," etc. (A player can win a game with a score of 150 while his opponent has scored but two fouls. The final score would read 150 to -2.)

If a player fouls on a shot that has not pocketed a ball, the point penalty is deducted from his score at the end of the previous inning. If a player fouls and pockets a ball on the same shot, that ball is spotted (not scored) and the point penalty is deducted from his score at the end of the previous inning.

———— EQUAL OFFENSE ————

Except when clearly contradicted by these additional rules,
the **General Rules of Pocket Billiards** apply.

TYPE OF GAME: Equal Offense is a game in which each player shoots until he misses a shot, fouls or pockets the maximum amount of balls allowed for the inning. The winner is determined by the total inning score (similar to bowling). Based on **14.1 Continuous**, the game is ideal for leagues, tournaments, handicapping and averaging; fair, fun and interesting for beginners as well as the advanced player. Although copyrighted by Jerry Briesath, he has placed no restrictions on its use.

PLAYERS: Any number.

BALLS USED: Standard set of objects balls 1-15, plus *cue ball*.

THE RACK: Standard *triangle* rack; balls placed entirely at random. The balls are racked at the beginning of each inning for each player.

OBJECT OF THE GAME: To *score* more total points than opponent(s) in a predetermined number of innings (200 points in 10 innings maximum).

SCORING: Any legally pocketed ball counts one point for shooter.

OPENING BREAK: At the start of each player's inning, he has a *free break* (no special balls to cushion or other requirements once break stroke commences, and a jumped or *scratched* cue ball is without penalty). Any balls pocketed on the break are spotted, and player then begins shooting with object balls in position and *cue ball in hand behind the head string.* The *opening break* takes place at the start of every inning of each player (10 times per match in Championship play for each player).

RULES OF PLAY:

1. Player may shoot any ball he chooses, but before he shoots must designate an object ball and a *called pocket.* He need not indicate *kisses, caroms, combinations* or *cushions,* (none of which are illegal). A legally pocketed ball entitles the shooter to continue at the table until he fails to pocket a *called ball,* or until he has scored the maximum total per inning permissable (20 points in championship play).

2. Player is entitled to any additional balls pocketed on a shot, as long as he pockets his called ball.

3. Shooting order for subsequent innings is determined by the scoring results of preceding innings – player with the highest score shooting first. In the event of a tie inning, the order does not change.

4. If players are tied for high match total (10 inning) score, additional innings are played by each tied player with the first player posting a superior score to his opponent(s), in an equal number of innings, being the winner ("sudden death").

JUMPED OBJECT BALLS: All spotted; no penalty. Player remains at the table if he has legally pocketed a called ball.

CUE BALL AFTER JUMP OR SCRATCH: Does not apply to Equal Offense, since a jumped or scratched cue ball ends player's inning, and all players' innings begin with the opening break.

PENALTY FOR FOULS: No point penalty; player's inning ends.

SOME VARIATIONS: For purposes of scheduling, handicapping, etc., variations can be made as follows:

1. A given number of misses or *fouls* may be allowed per inning (use 14.1 Continuous rules for "Cue Ball After Jump or Scratch").

2. Maximum number of balls per inning permissable may be increased or decreased.

3. Number of innings constituting a *match* may be increased or decreased.

4. Each player's inning may be restricted by a time limit.

5. Combinations of any of the variations above may be utilized, and may be applied in a non-uniform manner as a means of handicapping players.

6. As an exercise for beginners to progress in finding patterns of play, three chances should be allowed (two misses, *cue ball in hand*) to reach a score of 15. an intermediate player should be allowed two chances. The ten inning perfect score would thus be 150.

7. Third miss ends player's inning.

SIX BALL

Except when clearly contradicted by these additional rules,
the **General Rules of Pocket Billiards** apply.

TYPE OF GAME: Six Ball is a variation of **Rotation** in which the lowest numbered ball on the table must always be the players first cue ball contact. If a player complies, any pocketed ball counts. For example, if a player strikes the 1 ball legally, which then caroms into the 6 ball and causes it to be pocketed, that player wins the game. It's fast, and with only six object balls on the table, single inning racks are very common!

PLAYERS: 2 or more, though 2 players are generally preferred.

BALLS USED: Object balls 1-6, plus *cue ball.*

THE RACK: Triangle rack (rows of 1-2-3) with the 1 ball on the *foot spot,* and the 6 ball in the center of the rear row. All other balls placed entirely at random.

OBJECT OF THE GAME: To legally pocket the 6 ball.

SCORING: The balls have no point value. The player legally pocketing the 6 ball is credited with a game won.

OPENING BREAK: The starting player must (1) make an *open break,* or (2) legally pocket an object ball. If he fails to do so, the incoming player has choice of (1) *cue ball in hand behind the head string* and object balls in position, or (2) having the balls reracked and shooting the opening break shot himself.

RULES OF PLAY:

1. A legal shot requires that the cue ball's first contact be with the lowest numbered ball on the table. A player must then (1) pocket a ball, or (2) cause the cue ball or any object ball to contact a cushion. Failure to do so is a foul.

2. A legally pocketed ball entitles a shooter to remain at the table until he fails to pocket a ball on a legal shot.

3. When a player legally pockets a ball, he must shoot again. He may not call a *safety* and spot a legally pocketed object ball.

4. It is a loss of game if a player commits three *successive fouls.*

ILLEGALLY POCKETED BALLS: All spotted, no penalty, (Common Option, coin-operated play: None spotted except *game ball.*)

JUMPED OBJECT BALLS: All spotted; no penalty.

CUE BALL AFTER JUMP OR SCRATCH: Incoming player has *cue ball in hand.*

PENALTY FOR FOULS: Incoming player is awarded *cue ball in hand.* However, if a 3rd consecutive foul Rule of Play #4 provides for a penalty of loss of game.

SEVEN BALL

Except when clearly contradicted by these additional rules,
the **General Rules of Pocket Billiards** apply.

TYPE OF GAME: Seven Ball is a new, speedy rotational game designed to meet the time requirements of television. Averaging only about three minutes per game because contestants shoot at the same seven object balls, it permits players to show skills in making *combination* and *carom* shots, defensive shots and placement. At the same time, it is attractive to players of moderate skills, and readily adapts to handicapping by limiting the number of pockets in which the better contestant can legally pocket the game-winning 7 ball. Any nationwide commercial use of this game (patent pending) should be cleared in advance with Big Fights, Inc., 9 East 40th St., New York, New York 10016.

PLAYERS: 2 (or 2 teams)

BALLS USED: Object balls numbered 1-7, plus *cue ball.*

Seven Ball Rack

Diagram No. 4

THE RACK: A special circular rack has been designed for this game. A standard *diamond* rack (as used in **Nine Ball**) may also be used by turning it sideways.

The balls are racked in a circle on the *foot spot*, with the 1 ball at the apex (12 o'clock) and the balls increasing numerically 1-6 (clockwise in a circle) with the 7 ball in the middle of the circle. (See Diagram No. 4).

OBJECT OF THE GAME: To legally pocket the 7 ball.

SCORING: The balls have no point value. The player legally pocketing the 7 ball is credited with a game won.

OPENING BREAK: The starting player must (1) make an *open break*, or (2) legally pocket an object ball. If he fails to do so, incoming player has choice of foul Penalty #1, or having the balls reracked and shooting the opening break shot himself. In subsequent games loser breaks.

RULES OF PLAY:

1. A legal shot requires that the cue ball's first contact be with the lowest numbered ball on the table. A player must then (1) pocket a ball, or (2) cause the cue ball or any object ball to contact a *cushion*. Failure to meet these requirements is a *foul* and foul Penalty #2 applies.

2. A legally pocketed ball entitles a shooter to remain at the table until he fails to pocket a ball on a legal shot.

3. After a legal opening break, opponent chooses which side of the table (any of the three pockets on one side) into which he will pocket the 7 ball. Balls 1-6 may be pocketed on either side of the table.

4. Pocketing the 7 ball on a fair opening break wins the game.

5. Any violation of **General Rules** results in Penalty #2.

LOSS OF GAME: A player loses the game if he commits any of the following infractions: (a) pockets the 7 ball in a non-assigned pocket after the break, (b) scratches when the 7 ball is his legal object ball, (c) pockets the 7 ball on an illegal shot; (d) misses when the 7 ball is his object ball (optional–an alternative is to assess Foul Penalty #2); (e) commits three successive fouls.

ILLEGALLY POCKETED OBJECT BALLS: All *spotted*, Penalty #2 applies. (Optional for coin-operated tables: all balls remain pocketed; Penalty #2 applies.)

JUMPED OBJECT BALLS: All spotted, no penalty.

CUE BALL AFTER JUMP OR SCRATCH: Incoming player has cue ball in hand.

PENALTY FOR FOULS: No point penalty. (1) Incoming player has *cue ball in hand behind the head string* and object balls in position, but if the lowest numbered object ball is also behind head string it must be spotted (2) *cue ball in hand* anywhere on the table.

VARIATION: Players of unequal ability may be handicapped by assigning them more or less pockets in which they can play the 7 ball. It is suggested that more skilled players shoot the 7 ball into the side pocket on their side of the table. Players may also agree that the 7 ball can be pocketed anywhere on table.

TEN BALL

Except when clearly contradicted by these additional rules,
the **General Rules of Pocket Billiards** apply.

TYPE OF GAME: Tenball is a variation of **Rotation** in which a rack of just ten object balls is employed. As you will discern from the following rules, it is virtually the same game as **Nineball**, but with the extra ball adding both additional difficulty and generally fewer balls being pocketed on the opening break (particularly the ten-, or game-ball). Still, accomplished players turn it into a fast, action packed game!

PLAYERS: 2 or more, though 2, 3, or 4 is generally preferred.

BALLS USED: *Object balls* 1-10, plus *cue ball*.

THE RACK: *Triangle rack* truncated by removal of the rear row of balls (rows 1-2-3-4) with the 1 ball on the *foot spot*, and the 10 ball in the center of the row-of-3; other balls may be placed entirely at random.

OBJECT OF THE GAME: To legally pocket the 10 ball.

SCORING: The balls have no point value. The player legally pocketing the 10 ball is credited with a game won.

OPENING BREAK: The starting player must either (1) make an *open break*, or (2) legally pocket an object ball. If he fails to do so, incoming player has choice of (1) *cue ball in hand behind the head string* and object balls in position, or (2) having the balls reracked and shooting the opening break shot himself.

RULES OF PLAY:

1. A legal shot requires that the cue ball's first contact with a ball is with the lowest numbered ball on the table. AND THEN either (1) pocket a ball, or (2) cause the cue ball or any object ball to contact a cushion. Failure to meet this requirement is a foul.

2. A legally pocketed ball entitles shooter to remain at the table until he fails to pocket a ball on a legal shot.

3. When a player legally pockets a ball, he must shoot again. He may not call a *safety* and spot a legally pocketed ball.

4. It is loss of game if a player commits three successive fouls.

ILLEGALLY POCKETED BALLS: All spotted, no penalty. (Common option, coin-op play: None spotted except the game ball, no penalty.)

JUMPED OBJECT BALLS: All spotted, no penalty. (Common option, coin-op play: None spotted except the game ball, no penalty.)

CUE BALL AFTER JUMP OR SCRATCH: Incoming player has *cue ball in hand*.

PENALTY FOR FOULS: Incoming player is awarded *cue ball in hand*. (Note: Rule of Play #4 calls for loss of game if the foul is a 3rd successive one.)

ROTATION

Except when clearly contradicted by these additional rules,
the **General Rules of Pocket Billiards** apply.

Rotation requires that the cue ball must contact the lowest numbered object ball first on each shot; any ball pocketed on a legal shot counts. It is not necessary to call balls or pockets. It is a formidable test of a player's imagination, shot-making and repertoire. Few games require more exacting position play.

PLAYERS: 2 or more, though 2 player games are generally preferred.

BALLS USED: Standard set of object balls 1-15, plus *cue ball*.

THE RACK: Standard *triangle* rack with the 1 ball on the foot spot, 2 ball on the right rear corner, 3 ball on the left rear corner, and 15 ball in the center. All other balls placed entirely at random.

OBJECT OF THE GAME: To score balls of greater total point value than opponent(s).

SCORING: Each legally pocketed object ball has a point value equal to its number. When a player's point total mathematically eliminates an opponent(s) from out scoring him (61 points in a two-player game), the game is ended. If two or more players tie for highest point total after all fifteen object balls have been pocketed, the tied player who legally pocketed the last object ball is credited with an extra tie-breaking point and wins the game.

OPENING BREAK: The starting player must (1) make an *open break*, or (2) legally pocket an object ball. If he fails to do so, the incoming player has the choice of (1) shooting with *cue ball in hand behind the head string* and object balls in position, or (2) having the balls reracked and shooting the opening break shot himself.

RULES OF PLAY:

1. A legal shot requires that the cue ball's first contact be with the lowest numbered ball on the table. A player must then (1) pocket a ball, or (2) cause the cue ball or any object ball to contact a cushion. Failure is a foul.

2. A legally pocketed ball entitles a shooter to remain at the table until he fails to pocket a ball on a legal shot. If necessary, a player is permitted only two legal safeties played by merely hitting that object ball (only) to the near cushion.

3. When a player legally pockets a ball, he must shoot again. He may not call a *safety* and spot a legally pocketed object ball.

4. When a player has the cue ball in hand behind the head string (as after a scratch) and the legal object ball is also behind the headstring, the object ball may be spotted on the foot spot at his request.

5. It is a loss of game if a player commits three *successive fouls*. In more than a two player game, balls pocketed by disqualified players remain off the table.

ILLEGALLY POCKETED BALLS: All spotted.

JUMPED OBJECT BALLS: All spotted; no penalty.

CUE BALL AFTER JUMP OR SCRATCH: Incoming player has cue ball in hand behind the head string.

PENALTY FOR FOULS: No point penalty. Incoming player has the option of (1) accepting the balls in position, or (2) requiring offending player to shoot again with the table in position (if cue ball is in hand behind the string it is so for either player), Rule of Play #5 takes precedence in the case of a third consecutive foul.

BANK POOL

Except when clearly contradicted by these additional rules,
the **General Rules of Pocket Billiards** apply.

TYPE OF GAME: In **Bank Pool**, each shot must be a *bank* of an object ball into at least one cushion before the ball is pocketed. "Straight-in" shots are not legal. It is by definition a demanding game, and fascinating to observe, particularly when the players are accomplished at the art of banking.

PLAYERS: 2, 3, 4 or 5 players, though 2 players are generally preferred.

BALLS USED: Standard set of object balls 1-15, plus *cue ball*.

THE RACK: Standard *triangle* rack; balls placed entirely at random.

OBJECT OF THE GAME: To score a greater number of balls than opponent(s).

SCORING: Each legally pocketed object ball is scored as one ball. In two-player games, the first player to score eight balls wins. In three-player games, the first player to score five balls wins. In four-player games, the first player to score four balls wins. In five-player games, the first scored ball (though credited to the shooter) is immediately *spotted*, and the player continues to shoot; the first player to score four balls wins.

OPENING BREAK: Starting player must make an *open break*. If he fails to do so, incoming player has choice of (1) accepting the table in position and shooting, or (2) having the balls reracked and shooting the opening break shot himself.

No balls may be scored on the *opening break*. If any balls are pocketed on a legal opening break shot, they are spotted and the breaker continues shooting.

RULES OF PLAY:

1. A legally pocketed ball entitles shooter to remain at the table until he fails to legally pocket a ball. Player may shoot any object ball, but must designate which ball, pocket and the cushion(s) that ball will contact. A legally pocketed ball must be driven into at least one cushion and rebounded into the *called pocket*.

2. A legally pocketed ball must be "cleanly" banked (i.e., no *kisses*, no *combinations*, or *caroms* involving the *object ball* are permitted). The cue ball may contact the object ball only once on a stroke.

3. On a legal scoring stroke, only the object ball is credited to the shooter. Any other balls pocketed on the same stroke do not count for the shooter, and may be subject to special spotting provisions regarding "Illegally Pocketed Balls."

4. When a player has the *cue ball in hand behind the head string* (as after a scratch) and all object balls are also behind the head string, the object ball nearest the head string may be spotted on the foot spot at his request. If two or more balls are an equal distance from the head string, the player may also designate which of the balls he desires to be spotted.

5. Cushion impact shall mean clear and distinct contact with a cushion by the object ball. Incidental contact with a cushion as the object ball approaches the *called pocket* shall not be considered an "extra" cushion(s) that would otherwise disqualify a legal shot. Rebounding of the object ball in the *jaws* of the pocket before dropping shall not be considered "extra" cushions unless otherwise designated by the player.

6. It is a loss of game if a player commits three *successive fouls*.

ILLEGALLY POCKETED BALLS: All spotted, no penalty. Special spotting rule: when in the course of a legal scoring stroke, an additional ball(s) is pocketed (or jumped off the table), spotting of the ball(s) is delayed until the shooter's inning ends. Should a player score the last ball on the table while any illegally pocketed or jumped balls are being held for delayed spotting, those balls are then spotted so the player may continue his inning.

JUMPED OBJECT BALLS: All spotted; no penalty. Special spotting rule for "Illegally Pocketed Balls" may also apply to jumped object balls.

CUE BALL AFTER JUMP OR SCRATCH: Incoming player has cue ball in hand behind the head string.

PENALTY FOR FOULS: The player committing the foul must spot one of his previously scored object balls for each foul committed. If a player fouls when he has no previously pocketed balls to spot up, he "owes" for such fouls, and must spot balls after each scoring inning until his "owed" fouls are eliminated. After fouls other than jumped cue ball or cue ball scratch, incoming player accepts the cue ball in position.

COMMON OPTION: In a simplified version of Bank Pool, players must designate only the ball and pocket (not the cushion order). Banks need not be "clean." Removing the cushion designation portions of Rule of Play #1, along with all of Rule #2 makes the above rules fully applicable to the simplified version of Bank Pool.

ONE POCKET

Except when clearly contradicted by these additional rules,
the **General Rules of Pocket Billiards** apply.

TYPE OF GAME: One Pocket is a unique game in which only two of the six pockets are employed for legal scoring. Any ball may be played and need not be called. What is required is that an object ball falls in the player's "target" pocket. It requires a wide variety of strokes, cue ball control, shot-making ability, patience and defensive strategy.

PLAYERS: 2, or 2 teams.

BALLS USED: Standard set of object balls 1-15, plus *cue ball*.

THE RACK: Standard *triangle* rack; balls placed entirely at random.

OBJECT OF THE GAME: To *score* a total of eight object balls in a player's target pocket before opponent.

SELECTION OF POCKETS: Prior to the opening break shot, starting player chooses one of the corner pockets on the foot end of the table as his target pocket; opponent then has the other foot end corner as his target pocket.

SCORING: A legally pocketed ball is scored as one ball for shooter. A ball pocketed in opponent's target pocket counts, unless the cue ball should scratch on the same shot. If the shot constitutes a foul rather than scratch, the opponent is allowed to keep the ball. Shooter's inning ends on a scratch or foul and any balls pocketed in shooter's pocket do not count on a foul or scratch. In addition, the shooter is penalized one ball for a foul or scratch.

OPENING BREAK: Starting player must (1) legally pocket an object ball into his target pocket, or (2) cause the cue ball to contact an object ball and after contact, the cue ball and at least one object ball must contact a cushion. Failure to do so is a foul.

RULES OF PLAY:

1. A legal shot requires that the cue ball contact an object ball and then (1) pocket an object ball, or (2) cause the cue ball or an object ball to contact a cushion. Failure to do so is a foul.

2. A legally pocketed ball in a target pocket entitles the shooter to remain at the table until he fails to pocket a ball in his target pocket on a legal shot. Player may shoot any object ball he chooses, and any ball pocketed in his target pocket on an otherwise legal stroke is a scored ball.

3. Balls pocketed in the four non-target pockets are "Illegally Pocketed Balls."

4. Balls pocketed by shooter in his opponent's target pocket are scored for the opponent, even if the stroke was a foul, but would not count if the cue ball would scratch or jump the table. However, if the stroke is not a foul and the shooter pockets a ball(s) in both target pockets, shooter's inning continues, with all legally pocketed balls scored to the appropriate player. If a shooter pockets a ball that brings the opponent's score to the number opponent needed to win the game, the shooter has lost.

5. When a player has the *cue ball in hand behind the head string* (as after a scratch) and all object balls are also behind the head string, the object ball nearest the head string may be *spotted* at his request. If two or more balls are an equal distance from the head string, the highest numbered ball is spotted.

6. Three *successive fouls* by the same player is loss of game.

ILLEGALLY POCKETED BALLS: All spotted. **Special spotting rules:** When a ball(s) is pocketed in a non-target pocket (or jumped off the table), spotting is delayed until the shooter's inning ends. Should a player legally score the last ball(s) on the table while illegally pocketed (or jumped) ball(s) are being held for delayed spotting, those balls are then spotted so the player may continue his inning.

JUMPED OBJECT BALLS: All spotted, no penalty.

CUE BALL AFTER JUMP OR SCRATCH: Incoming player has cue ball in hand behind the head string.

PENALTY FOR FOULS: The player committing the foul must spot one of his previously scored object balls for each foul committed. If a player who fouls has no previously pocketed balls to spot up, he "owes" for such fouls, and must spot balls after each scoring inning until his "owed" fouls are eliminated. After fouls other than jumped cue ball or cue ball scratch, incoming player accepts the cue ball in position.

THREE FOUL PENALTY: If a player scratches or fouls three consecutive turns at the table, it is a loss of game.

BREAKING SUBSEQUENT RACKS: If a "race" or set of games is being played as a match, loser of each game is starting player (shoots opening break) of succeeding game.

—— BASIC POCKET BILLIARDS ——

Except when clearly contradicted by these additional rules,
the **General Rules of Pocket Billiards** apply.

TYPE OF GAME: The game of **Basic Pocket Billiards** is a combination of the call shot aspects of **14.1 Continuous** and the "anything goes" character of **Fifteen Ball**. It is a game well-suited for "mixed" (beginners and accomplished players) play, particularly in a team mode.

PLAYERS: 2, or two teams.

BALLS USED: Standard set of object balls 1-15, plus *cue ball*.

THE RACK: Standard *triangle* rack; balls placed entirely at random.

OBJECT OF THE GAME: To score eight balls before opponent.

SCORING: Any legally pocketed ball is scored as one ball.

OPENING BREAK: Starting player must either (1) pocket a ball (does not have to call either ball or pocket), or (2) cause the cue ball to contact an object ball and then the cue ball and two object balls must contact a *cushion*.

Failure is a *breaking violation*; opponent can accept the *table in position* and shoot, or require that the balls be reracked and offending player repeat the *opening break* until the requirements are satisfied.

If starting player pockets a ball on the opening break, it is a legally pocketed ball if no *foul* or other violation is committed, and he continues at the table. On all subsequent shots, however, he must comply with all the "Rules of Play" below.

RULES OF PLAY:

1. A legally pocketed ball entitles shooter to continue at the table until he fails to pocket a ball on a legal shot. Player may shoot any ball he chooses, but before he shoots must designate a single ball that he will pocket; he needs **not** indicate into which pocket the ball will score, *kisses, caroms, combinations* or cushions (all of which are legal).

2. On all shots subsequent to the opening break, player must cause the cue ball to contact an object ball, and then (1) pocket an object ball, or (2) cause an object ball or the cue ball to contact a cushion. Failure to do so is a foul.

3. When a player has the *cue ball in hand behind the head string*, the object ball nearest the head string may be spotted on the foot spot at his request. If two or more balls are an equal distance from the head string, the player may designate which of the equidistant balls he desires to be spotted.

ILLEGALLY POCKETED BALLS: All *spotted*; no penalty.

JUMPED OBJECT BALLS: All spotted; no penalty.

CUE BALL AFTER JUMP OR SCRATCH: Incoming player has cue ball in hand behind the head string.

PENALTY FOR FOULS: One scored ball is returned to the table (spotted) by fouling player for each foul committed. If player who fouls has no previously pocketed balls to spot up, he "owes" for such fouls, and must spot balls after each scoring inning until his "owed" fouls are eliminated. After fouls other than cue ball jump or cue ball *scratch*, incoming player accepts the cue ball in position.

———— BOTTLE POOL ————

Except when clearly contradicted by these additional rules,
the **General Rules of Pocket Billiards** apply.

TYPE OF GAME: A truly unique pocket billiard game, **Bottle Pool** requires the use of an inexpensive but specially shaped and balanced leather or plastic container ("bottle" or "*shaker bottle*"), shaped much like some disposable beverage bottles. The play of Bottle Pool combines the ball pocketing abilities of pocket billiards with the carom-making requirements of *carom* games.

PLAYERS: 2 or more.

BALLS USED: Object balls 1 and 2, plus *cue ball.*

THE RACK: No triangle needed; at the start of the game, the 1 ball is frozen to the *foot spot,* centered on the first diamond in from the racker's right corner pocket; the 2 ball is *frozen* to the *foot cushion,* centered on the first diamond in from the racker's left corner pocket; the bottle is placed open end down on the *center spot.* (See Diagram No. 7, Page 72.)

OBJECT OF THE GAME: To score exactly 31 points prior to opponent(s).

SCORING: There are five scoring possibilities. A player executing a legal stroke scores as follows:

(1) Pocketing the 1 ball: one point.

(2) Pocketing the 2 ball: two points.

(3) *Carom* of the cue ball on the two object balls: one point.

(4) Carom of the cue ball from an object ball(s) to the bottle which knocks the bottle onto its side: five points.

(5) Carom of the cue ball from an object ball(s) to the bottle which stands the bottle onto its base: automatic win of the game.

Should a player accomplish more than one scoring possibility on a shot, he scores for each; a single shot can result in a total of nine points scored.

Since **exactly** 31 points must be scored for victory (unless #5 above applies), a player must not exceed 31; if he does, his inning ends and his score becomes only the total by which he exceeded 31.

OPENING BREAK: No "break shot" as such. Beginning with *cue ball in hand behind the head string,* starting player must cause the cue ball to contact either the 1 ball or the 2 ball. If he fails to do so, incoming player can require that offending player repeat the opening shot until that requirement is satisfied.

RULES OF PLAY:

1. A legally executed scoring stroke entitles shooter to continue at the table until he fails to legally score on a shot, exceeds 31 points on a shot, causes an object ball to contact the bottle before the cue ball contacts the bottle (the entire shot is invalid and *inning* ends), or causes the bottle to be forced off the table or into a pocket (the entire shot is invalid and inning ends).

2. On all shots, player must cause the cue ball to contact an object ball. Failure to do so is a foul.

3. Cue ball must contact an object ball before it contacts the bottle. Failure to comply is a foul.

4. If player causes the bottle to be upset or, upended by an object ball, the shot is a foul.

5. Player loses the game if he fouls in each of three consecutive innings at the table.

REPLACING UPSET BOTTLE: Whenever the bottle is upset, it is replaced on the table, open end down, with the open end as close as possible to its position when the bottle came to rest. It is, of course, replaced prior to the next shot.

When the bottle is forced off the table or into a pocket (or into such position that the open end is over the pocket opening, making replacement as in the preceding paragraph impossible), the bottle is replaced on the center spot. If occupied, the head spot; if occupied, the foot spot; if occupied, hold out until center spot is vacant.

Bottle Pool

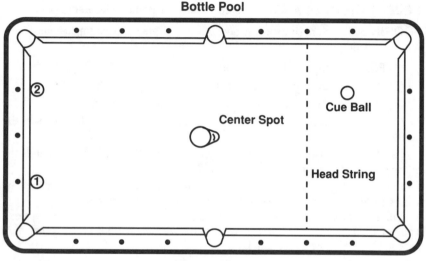

Diagram No. 7

ILLEGALLY POCKETED BALLS: All spotted; no penalty. (See "Special Spotting Rules" below.)

JUMPED OBJECT BALLS: All spotted; no penalty. (See "Special Spotting Rules" below.)

SPECIAL SPOTTING RULES: After each shot is completed, any pocketed object balls are spotted prior to the next shot. They are spotted in the positions as at the start of the game. If a ball or the bottle prevents the free placement of an object ball to be spotted, the object ball is spotted on the center spot; if that is also occupied, the object ball is then spotted on the head spot. If both object balls are being spotted, follow the above, first spotting the one ball, then the two ball.

CUE BALL AFTER JUMP OR SCRATCH: Incoming player has cue ball in hand behind the head string.

PENALTY FOR FOULS: One point is deducted from offender's score for each foul. After fouls other than cue ball jump or cue ball *scratch,* incoming player accepts the cue ball in position.

BOWLLIARDS

Except when clearly contradicted by these additional rules,
the **General Rules of Pocket Billiards** apply.

TYPE OF GAME: Bowlliards is a game that applies the scoring concepts of bowling to pocket billiards. It is one of the few games that can be quite interesting as a solitary exercise since, like bowling, there is perfect game score to strive toward, and a player can measure his improvement quite easily over the course of time playing Bowlliards.

PLAYERS: Any number.

BALLS USED: Any ten objects balls, plus *cue ball*.

THE RACK: Standard triangle position (front apex ball on *foot spot*), using a 1-2-3-4 rack configuration.

OBJECT OF THE GAME: To score a perfect score of 300 points in 10 frames (innings) in solitary play. In competition, to score a higher point total in 10 innings than opponent(s).

SCORING: Each legally pocketed ball is scored as one point, regardless of ball number. The points scored as per the "Rules of Play" below are treated exactly as is the pinfall in bowling.

OPENING BREAK: At the start of player's inning (frame), he has a *free break* (no special balls-to-cushion or other requirements once break stroke commences, and a jumped or *scratched* cue ball is without penalty). Any balls pocketed on the break are *spotted,* and player then follows his break by beginning scoring play with object balls in position and *cue ball in hand behind the head string*. (The opening break takes place at the start of every inning.)

RULES OF PLAY:

1. A legally pocketed ball entitles shooter to continue at the table until he fails to pocket a *called ball* on a shot, or until he has scored the maximum total per inning possible (10). Player may shoot any ball he chooses, but before he shoots, must designate a single ball that he will pocket and the pocket into which the ball will score; he need not indicate *kisses, caroms, combinations* or *cushions* (none of which are illegal).

2. Player has two chances to pocket the 10 possible balls of each frame. If player legally pockets ten consecutive balls on his first chance of a frame, that frame is completed and player scores the frame exactly as a strike in bowling. If player fails to pocket ten consecutive balls on his first chance, he takes his second chance immediately. If he succeeds in legally pocketing the remaining balls of the ten on his second chance, the frame is completed and player scores it exactly as a spare in bowling. If player fails to legally pocket all ten balls in two chances, the frame is then completed and is scored just as in bowling; a "strike" in the tenth inning earns two extra shots, a spare one extra shot.

3. If players tie for high game total in competition, additional extra innings are played alternately by the tied players, with the first player posting a superior score to that of his opponent(s) being the winner ("sudden death").

ILLEGALLY POCKETED BALLS: On the break, illegally pocketed balls are spotted prior to player beginning his scoring play (first chance of the frame). During scoring play, illegally pocketed balls are spotted.

JUMPED OBJECT BALLS: All spotted; no penalty.

CUE BALL AFTER JUMP OR SCRATCH: Only applies if occuring as player's first foul of a frame: player has cue ball in hand behind the head string to begin his second chance of the frame.

PENALTY FOR FOULS: One point is deducted from offender's score for each *foul*. If foul ends player's first chance of a frame, he has cue ball in hand behind the head string to begin his second chance of the frame.

BUMPER POOL

Rules and Regulations (Reprinted with permission of
The Valley Company, Bay City, Michigan)

1. Bumper Pool® is played by two players or by four as partners.

2. Each side has five red balls or five white balls, one of each color being a marked cue ball.

Bumper Pool

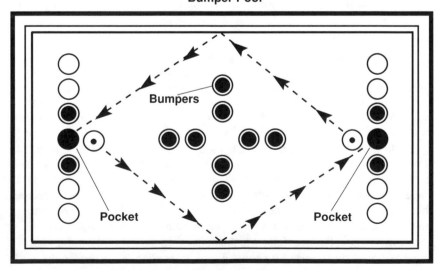

Diagram No. 8

3. To set up Bumper Pool®, place two red balls on each side of white cup (pocket) on markers, placing marked red ball directly in front of white cup. Place white balls in same position around the red cup (pocket).

4. Both players shoot marked ball at the same time, hitting first the side-cushion, banking the ball into or near his color cup. The player who plays his ball into or nearest his cup shoots again. Marked cue balls must be pocketed first. If a player sinks another ball before his marked ball is pocketed, his opponent may remove two of his own balls and drop them into his cup. In the event that both marked balls are pocketed on first shots each player takes one of remaining balls and spots it in front of cup and both shoot at same time, just as they did with marked balls. From there on they take turns beginning with the player who pockets his ball or is nearest to his cup.

5. A player receives another shot upon sinking his own color ball in his own color cup.

6. In the event that a player causes a ball to leave the table, his opponent may place this ball anywhere he wishes, and in addition can remove two of his own balls and drop them into his cup as an additional bonus.

7. If a player sinks one of his opponent's balls there is no penalty, but if he sinks one his own balls into his opponent's cup, or shoots one of his opponent's balls, his opponent may then drop two of his own balls into his cup.

8. No player is allowed to jump his ball over balls or bumpers in making shots. Penalty for this will be the same as in Rule Seven.

9. The first player or team to sink all five of their balls is the winner, except-ing that player forfeits game if he shoots his last ball into his opponent's cup.

10. The length of time that the winners may continue playing is governed by House Rule.

———————— COWBOY ————————

Except when clearly contradicted by these additional rules,
the **General Rules of Pocket Billiards** apply.

TYPE OF GAME: Cowboy is another game that combines carom and pocket billiards skill, and employs a very unusual set of rules. Certainly a change of pace game; how many games have you played in which the cue ball **must** be pocketed on a carom of the 1 ball on the last shot??!

PLAYERS: Any number.

BALLS USED: Object balls 1, 3 and 5, plus the *cue ball.*

THE RACK: No *triangle* needed; the 1 ball is placed on the *head spot*, the 3 ball on the *foot spot*, and the 5 ball on the *center spot*.

Cowboy Pocket Billiards

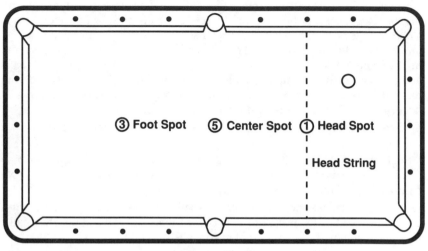

Diagram No. 9

OBJECT OF THE GAME: To score 101 points prior to opponent(s).

SCORING: The first ninety points exactly may be scored by any of these means on legal scoring strokes:

(1) pocketing any of the objects balls: points equal to the balls' numbers; and/or

(2) *carom* of the cue ball off two of the object balls: one point; and/or

(3) carom of the cue ball off the three object balls: two points.

Points 91 through 100 (exactly) must, and may only, be scored by execution of carom shots #2 and #3 above.

Points 101 (winning point) must be scored by caroming the cue ball off the 1 ball into a *called pocket* without the cue ball contacting any other object ball.

Should a player accomplish more than one scoring possibility permitted by these rules, he scores for each; thus a single shot can result in a total of 11 points scored.

OPENING BREAK: No "break shot" as such. Beginning with *cue ball in hand behind the head string*, starting player must cause the cue ball to contact the 3 ball first. If starting player fails to do so, incoming player has choice of (1) requiring starting player to repeat the opening shot, or (2) executing the opening shot himself.

RULES OF PLAY:

1. A legally executed shot, conforming to the requirements of "Scoring", entitles shooter to continue at the table until he fails to legally execute and score on a shot.

2. On all shots, player must cause the cue ball to contact an object ball, and then the cue ball or object ball must contact a *cushion*. Failure to do so is a foul.

3. At the completion of each shot, any pocketed object balls are *spotted* on their same positions as at the start of the game. If the appropriate position is occupied, the ball(s) in question remain off the table until the correct position is vacant after a shot. If, however, the 1 ball would be held out as a player with exactly 100 points is to shoot, the balls are all placed as at the start of the game, and the player shoots with cue ball in hand behind the head string.

4. When a player scores his 90th point, the shot must score the number of points exactly needed to reach 90; if the shot producing the 90th point also scores a point(s) in excess of 90 for the player, the shot is a *foul*.

5. When a player is playing for points 91 through 100 (which must all be scored on *caroms* solely), it is a foul to pocket an object ball on a shot.

6. When a player is playing for his 101st point, it is a foul if the cue ball is pocketed in a pocket other than the one called, of if the cue balls fails to contact the 1 ball, or if the cue ball contacts any other object ball.

7. When a player pockets the cue ball on an otherwise legal shot, and according to the special requirements given in "Scoring" for counting the 101st point, pocketing the cue ball on such a shot on the 101st point is not a foul.

8. Player loses the game if he fouls in each of three consecutive plays at the table.

ILLEGALLY POCKETED BALLS: All spotted per the provision of "Rules of Play" #3 (above), with no penalty, **except** in the special cases covered by the "Rules of Play" #4 & #5.

JUMPED OBJECT BALLS: All spotted; no penalty.

CUE BALL AFTER JUMP OR SCRATCH: Incoming player has cue ball in hand behind the head string.

PENALTY FOR FOULS: No point deduction, but any points scored on previous shots of the inning not scored, and player's inning ends. After fouls other than cue ball jump or cue ball *scratch,* incoming player accepts the cue ball in position.

CRIBBAGE

Except when clearly contradicted by these additional rules,
the **General Rules of Pocket Billiards** apply.

TYPE OF GAME: Cribbage Pocket Billiards derives its name from the fact that a score can only be made (with two exceptions) by pocketing a pair of balls in succession that add up to fifteen; a similarity exists with the popular card game of Cribbage. In a sense, it represents a combination of a call-shot game and a set-order game, and is a bit different and quite interesting to play.

PLAYERS: 2.

BALLS USED: Standard set of object balls 1-15 plus *cue ball*.

THE RACK: Standard *triangle* rack, with the 15 ball in the center; with the exception that no two of the three corner balls should add up to a total of fifteen points, all other balls may be placed entirely at random.

OBJECT OF THE GAME: To *score* five points (cribbages) out of a possible total of eight.

DEFINITION OF A CRIBBAGE: A cribbage is a pair of object balls, legally pocketed, numerically totaling 15. There are just these seven regular cribbages: 1-14, 2-13, 3-12, 4-11, 5-10, 6-9 and 7-8. No other ball combinations can be cribbages except that when all seven regular cribbages have legally pocketed, the 15 ball becomes a legal cribbage by itself.

SCORING: Each legally pocketed cribbage counts one point for scoring player.

OPENING BREAK: Starting player must cause the cue ball to contact an object ball, and then the cue ball and two object balls must contact a cushion. Failure to do so is a *breaking violation*; opponent has the choice of (1) requiring offending player to repeat the opening break (until requirements are satisfied), or (2) playing the opening break shot himself.

Starting player is not required to call his shot; if any balls are pocketed on the break shot, they accrue to him and he may continue at the table. Starting player generally uses an *open break*.

RULES OF PLAY:

1. To legally pocket a cribbage, the two balls must be pocketed in the same inning. When a player has legally pocketed a single ball on a shot, he must legally pocket the appropriate companion ball on his next shot, or it is a *foul*.

2. If a player scores a legal cribbage, he can continue his inning and attempt to score more cribbages in the same inning.

3. When not "on a cribbage," if a player pockets two or more balls on a shot that do not constitute a cribbage, he may next pocket any of the proper companion balls as he chooses, but must successively pocket each of those companion balls if he is to continue at the table. If he fails, it is a foul. If, while satisfying the

requirements of scoring companion balls, other ball(s) are incidentally pocketed, they likewise accrue to him; he must continue to complete one of the cribbages he is "on" on each successive stroke (though in no special order). Failure to do so is a foul; all balls of uncompleted cribbages are spotted.

4. When a ball is pocketed legally, but player fails to complete the cribbage legally during the same inning, the ball is spotted.

5. On all shots, player must cause the cue ball to contact an object ball and then either (1) pocket an object ball, or (2) cause an object ball or the cue ball to contact a cushion. Failure to do so is a foul.

6. Player loses the game if he commits three *successive fouls*.

7. If the 15 ball is pocketed before all the other cribbages have been legally pocketed, it is an illegally pocketed ball and is *spotted* immediately following the stroke (not inning) on which it was pocketed. No penalty.

8. When a player has the *cue ball in hand behind the head string* (as after a scratch) and all the object balls are also behind the head string, the object ball nearest the head string may be spotted on the foot spot at his request. If two or more balls are an equal distance from the head string, the player may also designate which of the equidistant balls he desires to be spotted.

ILLEGALLY POCKETED BALLS: All spotted; no penalty.

JUMPED OBJECT BALLS: All spotted; no penalty

CUE BALL AFTER JUMP OR SCRATCH: Incoming player has cue ball in hand behind the head string.

PENALTY FOR FOULS: Inning ends; no point or ball penalty (except per "Rule of Play" #6 above). Incoming player has the option of (1) accepting the table in position and shooting, or (2) shooting with cue ball in hand behind the head string.

CUT-THROAT

Except when clearly contradicted by these additional rules,
the **General Rules of Pocket Billiards** apply.

TYPE OF GAME: Cut-Throat (also known as Elimination) is a very popular game in social situations, rather than for serious competitive play. It is very enjoyable to play, fast and with simple rules. A perfect game when there are an odd number of participants available.

PLAYERS: 3 or 5.

BALLS USED: Standard set of object balls 1-15 plus *cue ball*.

THE RACK: Standard *triangle* rack with the 1 ball on the foot spot, and the 6 and 11 balls on the two corners; all other balls placed at random.

DETERMINATION OF GROUPS: In three-player game, starting player has the group of balls 1-5; second player has balls 6-10; third player has balls 11-15. In five-player game, starting player 1-3; second player 4-6; third 7-9; fourth 10-12; and fifth 13-15.

OBJECT OF THE GAME: To legally pocket your opponent(s) balls before the opponent(s) legally pocket your group of balls.

SCORING: Group balls have no point value. The player with a ball(s) still on the table, when all the other groups' balls are legally pocketed, wins the game.

OPENING BREAK: Starting player must make an *open break*. If he fails to do so, incoming player may either (1) accept the *table in position* and shoot, or (2) require that the balls be re-racked and shoot the opening break himself. All balls pocketed on a legal break remain pocketed.

RULES OF PLAY:

1. A legal shot requires that the cue ball's first contact be with the opponent(s) object ball. On all shots, player must cause the cue ball to contact an object ball and then either (1) pocket an object ball, or (2) cause an object ball and the cue ball to contact a cushion. Failure to meet these requirements is a foul. Any legally pocketed ball entitles shooter to continue at the table until he fails to pocket an object ball on a shot (Also see exception: "Rule of Play" #3.)

2. If player pockets any opponents' balls on an illegal shot, they are spotted; but if he pockets his own group balls on an illegal shot, they remain pocketed. If player pockets the last ball of his own group, whether or not on a legal shot, it remains pocketed and his inning ends.

3. When a player's last group ball is legally pocketed, he is eliminated from the shooting rotation. He remains eliminated for the duration of the game **unless** a foul is committed by a player still in the game; when a player is reinstated due to a foul, he resumes his normal position in the original order of play.

4. When a player has the *cue ball in hand behind the head string* (as after a scratch), and all balls of all opponents' groups are behind the head string, the object ball nearest the head string may, at the shooter's request, be spotted on the foot spot. If two or more balls are an equal distance from the head string, the player may designate which of the equidistant balls he desires to be spotted.

5. When successive games are being played, the order of play for the next game is the same as the order of final elimination in the preceding game. (First player eliminated breaks; winner shoots last; others in order of elimination.)

ILLEGALLY POCKETED BALLS: Opponents' group balls are *spotted;* no penalty. Shooter's group balls remain pocketed, no penalty.

JUMPED OBJECT BALLS: Same as "Illegally Pocketed Balls."

CUE BALL AFTER JUMP OR SCRATCH: Incoming player has cue ball in hand behind the head string.

PENALTY FOR FOULS: Shooter's inning ends. In addition, one ball from each of the opponents' groups that is off the table is brought back into play. Players who had been eliminated can be reinstated at any time until the game is over. If a player's group has no pocketed balls at the time of a foul by one of his opponents, then the penalty has no effect on that group or player; the penalty is not carried forward.

FIFTEEN BALL

Except when clearly contradicted by these additional rules,
the **General Rules of Pocket Billiards** apply.

TYPE OF GAME: Fifteen Ball is a basic game variation that does not require calling balls or pockets, and yet rewards good shot selection because scoring is based on the numerical values of the balls (numbers) as in **Rotation.** It is a game well-suited for developing skills at beginning and intermediate player levels.

PLAYERS: 2 or more, though 2 players are generally preferred.

BALLS USED: Standard set of object balls 1-15, plus *cue ball.*

THE RACK: Standard *triangle* rack with the 15 ball on the *foot spot;* other balls have no exact positions, but the higher numbered balls are placed at the front of the rack near the 15 ball, with the lower numbered balls near the back of the rack.

OBJECT OF THE GAME: To score balls of greater total point value than opponent(s).

SCORING: Each legally pocketed object ball has a point value equal to its number. Game ends when a player's point total mathematically eliminates opponent(s) [61 in a two player game]. If two or more players tie for highest point total, the tied player legally pocketing the last object ball is credited with the game.

OPENING BREAK: Starting player must either (1) pocket a ball (does **not** have to call either ball or pocket), or (2) cause the cue ball to contact an object ball, and then the cue ball and two object balls must contact a *cushion.* If he fails to do so, incoming player has choice of (1) accepting the *table in position* and shooting, or (2) having the balls re-racked and shooting the opening break shot himself, or (3) requiring offending player to repeat the opening break.

RULES OF PLAY:

1. Any ball pocketed on a legal shot entitles shooter to continue at the table until he fails to do so.

2. On all shots subsequent to the opening break, player must cause the cue ball to contact an object ball, and then either (1) pocket an object ball, or (2) cause an object ball or the cue ball to contact a cushion. Failure to do so is a foul.

3. When a player has the *cue ball in hand behind the head string* (as after a scratch) and all object balls are also behind the head string, the object ball nearest the head string may be spotted on the foot spot at his request. If two or more balls are an equal distance from the head string, the player may designate which of the equidistant balls he desires to be spotted.

ILLEGALLY POCKETED BALLS: All spotted; no penalty.

JUMPED OBJECT BALLS: All spotted; no penalty.

CUE BALL AFTER JUMP OR SCRATCH: Incoming player has cue ball in hand behind the head string.

PENALTY FOR FOULS: Three points are deducted from the offender's score for each foul committed. After fouls other than jumped cue ball or cue ball *scratch,* incoming player accepts the table in position.

FORTY-ONE

Except when clearly contradicted by these additional rules,
the **General Rules of Pocket Billiards** apply.

TYPE OF GAME: Forty-One Pocket Billiards is another game that is well suited for social play at parties or other gathering where players of mixed abilities will take part. Since no one knows what number *"pea"* is held by his opponent(s), it is difficult to play defensively. In addition, the rules are designed to greatly equalize all the players' chances. An unusual and interesting game!

PLAYERS: 2 to 15 (though 3, 4, or 5 are generally preferred).

BALLS USED: Standard set of object balls 1-15 plus *cue ball.* A set of fifteen numbered peas (or *"pills"*) and a *shake bottle* are also used.

THE RACK: Standard *triangle* rack with balls placed entirely at random.

DETERMINING PRIVATE NUMBERS: After the balls are racked but before play begins, each player is given a pea from the shake bottle containing the peas numbered from 1-15. The number of the pea is the player's private number and is kept secret.

OBJECT OF THE GAME: To score points which, when added to the player's private number, total exactly forty-one.

SCORING: Each legally pocketed ball has a point value equal to its number.

OPENING BREAK: Starting player must make an *open break*. He is not obligated to pocket a ball on the break shot; but if he fails to make a legal *open break,* it is a foul.

RULES OF PLAY:

1. Any ball(s) scored on a legal stroke count for the shooter. Players may shoot any ball and need not call ball, pocket or mode of shot.

2. A player is permitted only one shot or turn per inning, regardless of whether or not he scores.

3. An illegally pocketed ball is a foul, and does not score for the shooter.

4. On all shots, player must cause the cue ball to contact an object ball and then either (1) pocket an object ball, or (2) cause and object ball an the cue ball to contact a cushion. Failure to do so is a foul.

5. When a player has the *cue ball in hand behind the head string* (as after a scratch) and all object balls are also behind the head string, the object ball nearest the head string may be *spotted* on the foot spot at his request. If two or more balls are an equal distance from the head string, the player may designate which of the equidistant balls he desires to be spotted.

6. When player has a total count of forty-one, he must announce his victory and present his pea for confirmation prior to the next player shooting. If he fails to declare his forty-one total until the next player has shot, he must wait until his next turn to so declare. If, in the meantime, another player succeeds in attaining a legal total count of forty-one and properly declares, the latter player wins the game.

7. If a player totals more than forty-one points, he has "burst" and must so declare immediately (before next shooter plays). All balls the burst player had pocketed are spotted, and the burst player may request a new pea prior to his next turn if he so desires. Any player who bursts and does not declare it prior to the following player's shot is disqualified from further play in the game; if a two-player game, his opponent is automatically the winner.

8. If all balls are pocketed prior to any player attaining a total count of forty-one, the player whose count is closest to forty-one wins the game. If two or more players are tied for nearest to forty-one in this situation, the game is a tie.

ILLEGALLY POCKETED BALLS: All spotted; no penalty.

JUMPED OBJECT BALLS: All spotted; no penalty.

CUE BALL AFTER JUMP OR SCRATCH: Incoming player has cue ball in hand behind the head string.

PENALTY FOR FOULS: The player committing a foul must spot one of his previously scored object balls for each foul committed. If a player has no previously pocketed balls to his credit when he commits a foul, he is exempt from a penalty for that particular foul.

GOLF

Except when clearly contradicted by these additional rules,
the **General Rules of Pocket Billiards** apply.

TYPE OF GAME: There are probably more variations in **Golf** pocket billiards than any other game. This game is usually contested on Snooker tables, utilizing Snooker balls. Bearing a similar scoring technique as the sport of Golf, local and regional play flourishes.

PLAYERS: Any number.

BALLS USED: One numbered object ball for each player, plus *cue ball*.

THE RACK: Starting player's object ball is *spotted* on the *foot spot*.

OBJECT OF THE GAME: To successfully pocket the object ball in each of the six pockets in numerical pocket order (See Diagram # 10) in a lesser number of total shots (strokes) than opponent(s).

SCORING: Each shot is scored as one stroke added to player's score; each foul is scored as three strokes added to offending player's score.

Golf Pocket Billiards

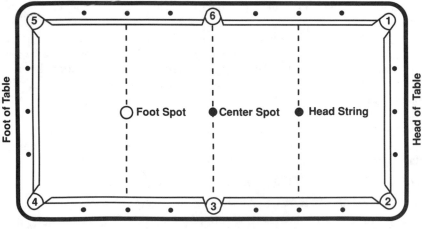

Diagram No. 10

OPENING BREAK: Starting player begins play with the cue ball on the *center spot* and the object ball on the foot spot. He must cause the object ball to contact the foot *cushion* on the first (opening break) shot. Failure is a *foul* and the balls are replaced in the starting positions, with offender repeating his attempt until he satisfies the requirement.

When starting player satisfies the opening break requirements, he continues play; opponent(s) do not yet begin. First player's objective is to pocket his object ball in pocket #1 in the least number of strokes possible. His total strokes, including any foul penalties incurred, are recorded as his score for hole #1.

Second player then begins his play for hole #1, with the same *opening break* requirements and ball positions applying to him. If there are more players, the routine is followed until the last player has completed hole #1; when that has been accomplished, the cue ball remains in position from the last player's final shot on hole #1.

SUBSEQUENT HOLES: After all players have pocketed their object ball in hole #1, the cue ball remains where it came to rest from the last player's final shot. The first player's object ball is spotted on the *foot spot*, and he begins play for hole #2. He need not *bank* the ball for this or any further holes, and the cue ball is kept in position throughout the remainder of the game (see below if jumped of scratched). Player #1 shoots successively until he has pocketed his ball in hole #2, with the other playersshooting similarly in regular order. Play continues thus all players have completed all six holes, playing in order, holes one through six.

RULES OF PLAY:

1. It is a foul to pocket the object ball in any pocket other than the one in which the player is attempting to score.

2. On all shots, player must cause the cue ball to contact the object ball and then either (1) pocket the object ball, or (2) cause the cue ball or object ball to contact a *cushion*. Failure to do so is a foul.

3. No more than three points are assessed for foul penalties on any one shot.

4. When the cue ball is in hand behind the *head string* (as after a *scratch*) and the object ball is also behind the head string, player may either (1) have the object ball spotted on the foot spot and shoot with the cue ball in hand behind the head string, or (2) have the cue ball spotted on the *head spot,* from where he may legally shoot at the object ball behind the head string.

5. It is a foul to jump the object ball off the table.

ILLEGALLY POCKETED BALLS: All spotted on the foot spot; three points added to offender's score.

JUMPED OBJECT BALLS: All spotted on the foot spot; three points added to the offender's score.

CUE BALL AFTER JUMP OR SCRATCH: Player continues play with the *cue ball in hand behind the head string* (NOTE the special option provided in Rule of Play #4).

PENALTY FOR FOULS: Three points are added to offender's score for each shot on which he commits a foul.

LINE-UP

Except when clearly contradicted by these additional rules,
the **General Rules of Pocket Billiards** apply.

TYPE OF GAME: Line-Up is a forerunner of **14.1 Continuous.** This is how they did it way back then!

PLAYERS: 2.

BALLS USED: Standard set of object balls numbered 1-15, plus *cue ball.*

THE RACK: Standard *triangle* rack with the front apex ball on the *foot spot,* 1 ball on the rack's right corner, 5 ball on left corner; other balls placed at random.

OBJECT OF THE GAME: To score the predetermined point total (usually 150 in tournaments, or any agreed upon total) for game prior to opponent.

SCORING: Any ball legally pocketed counts one point for shooter.

OPENING BREAK: Starting player must pocket a *called ball* or drive two object balls to a *cushion.* If he fails to do so, he is assessed a two point penalty. Incoming player may accept the *table in position* and shoot, or require that offender repeat the opening break until the requirements are satisfied. Each successive failure is a two point penalty for offending player.

RULES OF PLAY:

1. A legally pocketed ball entitles shooter to continue at the table until he fails to pocket a called ball on a shot. Player may shoot any ball he chooses, but before he shoots, must designate the ball he will pocket and the pocket into which the ball will score; he need indicate no other detail.

2. On all shots, player must cause the cue ball to contact an object ball and then either (1) pocket an object ball, or (2) cause the cue ball or any object ball to contact a cushion. Failure to do so is a *foul.*

3. A player may call a *safety* rather than an object ball if he so desires (for defensive purposes). Safety play is legal, but must comply with all applicable rules. Player's inning ends when safety is played, and pocketed balls are not scored. Any object ball pocketed on a called safety is *spotted.*

4. When the fifteenth ball of the rack has been pocketed, shooter records his scored balls from the rack. The balls are then spotted, and player continues shooting, playing the cue ball from where it came to rest after preceding shot, before the balls were spotted. (If player misses or fouls during the rack, he records his score and incoming player shoots, accepting the table in position.)

ILLEGALLY POCKETED BALLS: All spotted, no penalty.

JUMPED OBJECT BALLS: All spotted, no penalty.

CUE BALL AFTER JUMP OR SCRATCH: Incoming player has *cue ball in hand behind the head string* (unless the foul was a third successive foul; see "Successive Fouls Penalty").

PENALTY FOR FOULS: One point is deducted from offender's score for each foul committed, **unless** the foul is a third *successive foul* (see "Successive Fouls Penalty"). After fouls other than cue ball jump, cue ball *scratch,* or third *successive foul,* incoming player accepts the table in position.

SUCCESSIVE FOULS PENALTY: If a player commits three successive fouls, he is penalized one point for each foul, and an additional deduction of fifteen points. The balls are reracked and offending player is required to break the balls under the requirements of the opening break.

—————— MR. AND MRS. ——————

Except when clearly contradicted by these additional rules,
the **General Rules of Pocket Billiards** apply.

TYPE OF GAME: Mr. and Mrs. (also called Boy Meets Girl) is a game that combines the general forms of **Rotation** and **Basic Pocket Billiards**. The rules are different for players of widely differing skill levels.

PLAYERS: Any number from two to six.

BALLS USED: Standard set of object balls numbered 1-15, plus *cue ball.*

THE RACK: Standard *triangle* rack with the one ball on the *foot spot,* 2 ball on racker's right corner, 3 ball on left corner, 15 ball in the center. All other balls are placed at random.

OBJECT OF THE GAME: To score balls of greater total point value than opponent(s).

SCORING: Each legally pocketed object ball has a point value equal to its number. Game ends when a player's point total mathematically eliminates opponents(s) – 61 points in a two-player game. If two or more players tie for highest point total, the tied player that legally pocketed the last object ball is credited with a game won.

OPENING BREAK: Starting player must cause the cue ball's first contact to be with the 1 ball. If starting player fails to meet this requirement, incoming player has the choice of (1) accepting the *table in position* and shooting, or (2) requiring that the balls be reracked and offending player repeat the *opening break.*

RULES OF PLAY:

1. A legally pocketed ball entitles shooter to continue at the table until he fails to legally pocket a ball.

2. On all shots, more skilled player must cause the cue ball's first contact with a ball to be with the lowest numbered object ball on the table and then either (1

pocket a ball, or (2) cause the cue ball or any object ball to contact a *cushion*. Failure to do so is a foul.

3. Less skilled player may shoot any ball he chooses, regardless of number. He need not call ball, pocket or mode of shot. Any ball pocketed on a legal shot is a scored ball.

4. Player loses game if he commits three *successive fouls*. If more than a two-player game, balls previously pocketed by disqualified player remain off the table.

5. When a skilled player has the *cue ball in hand behind the head string* (as after a *scratch*) and the legal object ball is also behind the head string, the object ball may be spotted on the foot spot at his request.

6. When a less skilled player has the cue ball in hand behind the head string (as after a scratch) and all of the object balls are also behind the head string, the object ball nearest the head string may be spotted at his request. If two or more object balls are an equal distance from the head string, he may also designate which of the equidistant object balls he desires to be spotted.

ILLEGALLY POCKETED BALLS: All spotted, no penalty.

JUMPED OBJECT BALLS: All spotted, no penalty.

CUE BALL AFTER JUMP OR SCRATCH: Incoming player has cue ball in hand behind the head string.

PENALTY FOR FOULS: No point penalty. If foul is other than jumped cue ball or cue ball scratch, incoming player accepts the cue ball in position. A third consecutive foul by the same player is loss of game.

ODDBALL

Except when clearly contradicted by these additional rules,
the **General Rules of Pocket Billiards** apply.

TYPE OF GAME: This variation of **Oddball** is one of the more interesting team games of pocket billiards. For four players, it is based on Rotation playing requirements, but with its own scoring methodology that make it unique. The four players compete as two teams of two, so varied playing abilities can be accommodated through appropriate pairings on the teams. It can also be played by 2 individuals.

PLAYERS: Four, in two teams of two. (Teams can be larger if desired, but the best game is with 2-player teams.)

BALLS USED: Standard set of object balls 1 through 15 plus cue ball.

THE RACK: Standard triangle rack with the one ball on the foot spot, the two ball on the racker's right corner, the three ball on the left corner, and the fifteen ball in the center; other balls may be at random, or at racking player's discretion.

OBJECT OF THE GAME: To score 21 points prior to opposing team.

SCORING: Each legally pocketed ball contributes to the pocketing team's point total as follows: each odd-numbered object ball, 1 (one) point; each even-numbered object ball, O (no) points. In addition, 2 (two) points are earned by the team that legally pockets 61 or more points during each rack of play, computed by adding the numerical value of all balls (even and odd). (If the teams tie 60-60 in this end-of-rack computation, each earns one [1] point.) Thus there are ten (10) points scored during each rack of play. A running score is marked and kept after each rack of play. A game (to 21 points) can take between three and five racks of play. When a team scores its 21st legal point (previous points plus currently scored), it is the winner of the game.

OPENING BREAK: Starting player must make an *Open Break.* If he fails to do so, incoming player has the choice of either (1) requiring that the balls be re-racked and the offending player repeat the break shot, or (2) accepting the table in position and shooting, or (3) having the balls re-racked and shooting the opening break shot himself. The above requirements apply to the opening break shot of each successive rack played during a game.

RULES OF PLAY:

1. A legally pocketed ball entitles shooter to continue at the table until he fails to so pocket a ball on a shot.

2. On all shots, the cue ball's first contact with a ball must be with the lowest numbered object ball on the table and then the shot must (1) pocket a ball, or (2) cause the cue ball or any object ball to contact a cushion. Failure to do so is a foul.

3. A player legally pocketing a ball must shoot again; no nullifying safeties.

4. If only even numbered object balls remain on the table, and they can have no effect on the 2-point award for most total points of all numbered balls, they are not pocketed; the rack is over and the player who pocketed the last ball of consequence is deemed to have pocketed all of the remaining (meaningless) balls.

5. Player who pocketed the last ball of the preceding rack becomes the starting player for the next rack of that game.

6. Rotation of players must remain the same during all necessary racks of a game; once established, the rotation must remain the same until the game is over.

7. When a player has the *Cue Ball In Hand Behind the String* (as after a *scratch*) and the legal object ball at that time is in the kitchen, the object ball may be spotted on the foot spot at his request.

8. Player's team loses the game if he fouls in each of three consecutive plays at the table.

ILLEGALLY POCKETED BALLS: All spotted, no penalty.

JUMPED OBJECT BALLS: All spotted, no penalty.

CUE BALL AFTER JUMP OR SCRATCH: Incoming player has *Cue Ball In Hand Behind the String.*

PENALTY FOR FOULS: No point penalty. Incoming player has choice of either (1) accepting the table in position and shooting, or (2) requiring offending player to shoot again with the table in position (if *Cue Ball Is In Hand Behind the String*, it is so for either player). Rule #8 takes precedence in the case of any 3rd consecutive foul.

──── ONE-AND-NINE BALL ────

Except when clearly contradicted by these additional rules,
the **General Rules of Pocket Billiards** apply.

TYPE OF GAME: One-And-Nine Ball pocket billiards is actually team **Rotation**, with the partners not determined until after play of each game (rack) is partially completed. It is quite workable when four players do not wish to settle on permanent partners over the course of numerous games during a playing session. It makes for an interesting and unusual four-player game.

PLAYERS: 4.

DETERMINATION OF PARTNERS: The four players are paired into two teams during the play of each game. The player legally pocketing the 1 ball is automatically the partner of the player who legally pockets the 9 ball; if the 9 ball is pocketed by the same player that scored the 1 ball, then the partner is the player who legally pockets the 10 ball; if the same, then the 11 ball, etc.; if same player pockets all balls counting up through the 15 ball, then the partner is the player who pocketed the 8 ball; if the same, the 7 ball, etc. If one player pockets all fifteen balls, he wins as a one-player team, while the three other players lose as a three-player team.

BALLS USED: Standard set of object balls numbered 1-15, plus *cue ball.*

THE RACK: Standard *triangle* rack with 1 ball on the foot spot, 2 ball on the racker's right corner, 3 ball on the left corner, 9 ball in center. All other balls placed at random.

OBJECT OF THE GAME: To score, as a team, balls of greater total point value (at least 61) than opposing team.

SCORING: Each legally pocketed object ball has a point value equal to its number. Game ends when a team's point total reaches 61 or more. If the teams tie with 60 points each, the team whose player legally pocketed the last object ball is credited with a tie-breaking point and wins the game.

OPENING BREAK: Starting player must make an *open break*. If he fails to do so, incoming player has choice of (1) *cue ball in hand behind the head string* and object balls in position, or (2) having the balls reracked and shooting the opening break shot himself.

RULES OF PLAY:

1. A legally pocketed ball entitles shooter to remain at the table until he fails to legally pocket a ball on a shot.

2. On all shots, the cue ball's first contact must be with the lowest numbered object ball on the table and he must either (1) pocket a ball, or (2) cause the cue ball or any object ball to contact a *cushion*. Failure to do so is a *foul*.

3. A player legally pocketing a ball must shoot again. He may not call a *safety* and *spot* a pocketed object ball.

4. When a player has the cue ball in hand behind the head string (as after a scratch) and the legal object ball at that time is also behind the head string, the object ball may be spotted on the *foot spot* at his request.

ILLEGALLY POCKETED BALLS: All spotted, no penalty.

JUMPED OBJECT BALLS: All spotted, no penalty.

CUE BALL AFTER JUMP OR SCRATCH: Incoming player has cue ball in hand behind the head string.

PENALTY FOR FOULS: No point penalty. Incoming player has choice of either (1) accepting the *table in position* and shooting, or (2) requiring offending player to shoot again with the table in position. A team loses the game if its partners together commit three *successive fouls*.

——— ONE BALL ———

Except when clearly contradicted by these additional rules,
the **General Rules of Pocket Billiards** apply.

TYPE OF GAME: One Ball pocket billiards is a unique, single rack game, with only one scoring ball in the rack.

PLAYERS: 2.

BALLS USED: Standard set of object balls numbered 1-15, plus *cue ball* (or any 14 object balls and a single distinctive object ball, plus cue ball).

THE RACK: Standard *triangle* rack with front apex ball on the *foot spot,* and the 1 ball (or the single distinctive object ball) in the center. Other balls are placed at random.

OBJECT OF THE GAME: To legally pocket the 1 ball.

SCORING: Object balls have no point value. The player legally pocketing the 1 ball is credited with a game won.

OPENING BREAK: Starting player must either (1) designate a pocket into which a ball (any ball) will drop and successfully accomplish the shot, or (2) cause the cue ball to contact an object ball and then a *cushion*, plus cause two object balls to contact a cushion. Failure to meet one of these requirements is a *breaking violation;* opponent has the choice of either (a) accepting the *table in position,* or (b) having the balls reracked and requiring offending player to repeat the opening break. That choice continues until opening break is legally executed, or until opponent accepts the table in position. If starting player commits three consecutive breaking violations, it is loss of game.

RULES OF PLAY:

1. A legally pocketed ball entitles shooter to continue at the table until he fails to pocket a ball on a legal shot.

2. A legally pocketed ball is **any** ball (except the 1 ball) in a *called pocket.* He need not call *combinations, kisses, caroms,* etc., all of which are legal.

3. Prior to the opening break, starting player selects and announces which of the side pockets he desires as his target pocket for the 1 ball. Opponent then has the other side pocket as his target pocket for the 1 ball.

4. The 1 ball may be legally pocketed when the player calls "1 ball" prior to his stroke and drops it in his target pocket.

5. On all shots, player must cause the cue ball to contact an object ball and then either (1) pocket an object ball, or (2) cause the cue ball or an object ball to contact a cushion. Failure to do so is a *foul.*

6. When a player has the *cue ball in hand behind the head string* (as after a *scratch*) and all object balls are also behind the head string, the object ball nearest the head string may be spotted on the foot spot at his request. If two or more balls are an equal distance from the head string, the player may designate which of the equidistant balls he desires to be spotted.

ILLEGALLY POCKETED BALLS: All spotted, no penalty.

JUMPED OBJECT BALLS: All spotted, no penalty.

CUE BALL AFTER JUMP OR SCRATCH: Incoming player has cue ball in hand behind the head string.

PENALTY FOR FOULS: No point penalty. After fouls other than cue ball jump or cue ball scratch, incoming player accepts the table in position. Player loses the game if he commits three *successive fouls.*

——————— PEA (KELLY) POOL ———————

Except when clearly contradicted by these additional rules,
the **General Rules of Pocket Billiards** apply.

TYPE OF GAME: **Pea** (or Kelly) **Pool** is an old favorite among pocket billiard players who enjoy a group game in which the competitors play individually, and which entails a bit of luck (not so much in the actual play but rather in the *pea* or *pill* each player receives during each game). The game is very popular since it can accommodate players of widely differing levels of ability.

PLAYERS: 2 or more, with the best game being from four to six.

BALLS USED: Standard set of object balls numbered 1-15, plus *cue ball.* A set of fifteen number peas (or "pills") and a *shake bottle* are also used.

THE RACK: Standard *triangle* rack with 1 ball on the *foot spot,* 2 ball on racker's right corner, 3 ball on left corner. All other balls placed at random.

DETERMINING PRIVATE NUMBERS: After the balls are racked, but before play begins, each player is given a pea from the shake bottle (containing the peas numbered 1-15). The number of the pea is the player's private number and is kept secret.

OBJECT OF THE GAME: To legally pocket the object ball with the numerical value equivalent to the player's private number.

SCORING: No point value for object balls except the ball equivalent to pocketing player's private number; when a player legally pockets that object ball, he wins the game. (**Option**: Game is played until a player legally pockets "his own" ball and wins, as above, he receives two points from each player for winning the game. In addition when any player's "private number ball" is legally pocketed by any player other than himself, the pocketing player receives one point and the player whose ball was pocketed loses one point. Players whose private number balls have been pocketed by other players continue to shoot in the regular rotation, but if a player fails to announce that his object ball was pocketed by another player prior to a subsequent shot being taken, the offending player is disqualified from further play during the game, and the forfeiture of points to the pocketing player is increased from one to two. If no player succeeds in pocketing his private number ball, the game ends when the last private number ball is pocketed, and another game is played with all point values doubled and player who pocketed the last private number ball being the starting player.)

OPENING BREAK: Starting player must make an *open break.* If he fails to do so, incoming player has choice of either (1) *cue ball in hand behind the head string* and *table in position,* or (2) having the balls reracked and shooting the opening break shot himself.

RULES OF PLAY:
   1. A legally pocketed ball entitles shooter to continue at the table until he fails to legally pocket a ball.

2. On all shots, the cue ball's first contact must be with the lowest numbered object ball on the table and then must either (1) pocket a ball, or (2) cause the cue ball or any object ball to contact a *cushion*. Failure to do so is a *foul*.

3. A player legally pocketing a ball must shoot again. He may not call a *safety* and *spot* a pocketed ball.

4. When a player has the cue ball in hand behind the head string (as after a *scratch*) and the legal object ball is also behind the head string, the object ball may be spotted on the foot spot at his request.

ILLEGALLY POCKETED BALLS: All spotted, no penalty.

JUMPED OBJECT BALLS: All spotted, no penalty.

CUE BALL AFTER JUMP OR SCRATCH: Incoming player has cue ball in hand behind the head string.

PENALTY FOR FOULS: No point penalty. Incoming player has choice of either (1) accepting the table in position and shooting, or (2) requiring offending player to shoot again (if cue ball is in hand behind the string, it is so for either player).

———— AMERICAN SNOOKER ————

TYPE OF GAME: American Snooker is a "cousin" of Snooker as it is played widely around the world; the rules giving it a distinct orientation toward the structure of many American pocket billiard games. It is generally played on either 5 x 10 or 6 x 12 Snooker tables, with cushions that are more narrow than other pocket billiard tables, and curve smoothly into the pocket openings. The balls used are either 2-$\frac{1}{16}$" or 2-$\frac{1}{8}$" diameter. (See **BCA Specifications**.)

PLAYERS: 2.

BALLS USED: Set of Snooker balls: fifteen object balls that are not numbered and are solid red (called reds), six object balls that may or may not be numbered (called colors) and a cue ball. Point values for object balls: yellow-2, green-3, brown-4, blue-5, pink-6, black-7.

THE RACK: Play begins with balls placed as in Diagram 11.

OBJECT OF THE GAME: To score a greater number of points than opponent.

SCORING: Points are scored in two ways; players are awarded points for fouls by the opponent (see "Penalty For Foul" below), and by legally pocketing reds and/or colors. Each legally pocketed red ball has a point value of one; each legally pocketed color ball has a point value as indicated ("Balls Used" above). Game ends when all balls have been pocketed, following the Rules of Play; if, however, only the black (7) ball is left on the table, the game ends with the first score or foul. If the players' scores are equal after that scoring, the black ball is spotted on its

American Snooker – 5x10 Table

Diagram No. 11

original position and the players lag for the choice of shooting at, or assigning opponent to shoot at the black ball with the *cue ball in hand within the D;* the first score or foul then ends the game.

OPENING BREAK: Starting player has cue ball in hand within the D. He must (1) cause the cue ball to contact a red ball prior to contacting a color, and (2) cause a red ball to contact a cushion or drop into a pocket, and (3) cause the cue ball to contact a cushion after it contacts a red ball. Failure to meet these requirements is a foul and a *breaking violation.* A foul is scored and incoming player has choice of (1) accepting the table and shooting, and (2) requiring offender to break again.

RULES OF PLAY:

1. A legally pocketed ball entitles shooter to continue at the table until he fails to legally pocket a ball.

2. On all shots, player must comply with the appropriate requirements of Rules #5 & #6, plus cause the cue ball or an object ball to contact a cushion or drop in a pocket after the cue ball has contacted a legal object ball (on ball). Failure to do so is a foul.

3. As long as reds are on the table, an incoming player (player taking his first shot of an inning) always has a red as his legal object ball (on ball).

4. Any red balls pocketed on a legal shot are legally pocketed balls; player need not call any particular red ball(s), pocket(s) or mode of pocketing.

5. When a player has a red ball as his "on ball" (required legal object ball), he must cause the cue ball's first contact to be with a red ball. He must cause the cue ball's first contact to be with a red ball. Failure to do so is a foul. Rule #2 also applies.

6. After a player has scored a red ball initially, his next legal object is a color, and as long as reds remain on the table he must alternate his play between reds and

colors (though within each group he may play ball of his choice). When reds remain on the table and a color is his object, the player must (a) designate prior to shooting which color ball is his object (that specific color is then his "on ball"), and (b) cause the cue ball's first contact with a ball to be with that color ball. If player fails to meet these requirements, it is a foul. Rule #2 requirements also apply.

7. If player's on ball is a red, and he pockets a color, it is a foul.

8. If player's on ball is a color, and he pockets any other ball, it is a foul.

9. It is a foul if a player intentionally causes the cue ball to jump (rise from the bed of the table) by any means, if the jump is an effort to clear an obstructing ball.

10. While reds remain on the table, each pocketed color ball is spotted prior to the next stroke. (See "Spotting Balls" below for spotting rules.) If player shooting after a color has been spotted plays while that ball is incorrectly spotted (and opponent or referee calls it before two such shots have been taken), the shot taken is a foul. If such shooting player shoots twice after such error without it being announced by opponent or referee, he is free of penalty and continues shooting and scoring normally as though the spotting error simply had not occurred.

11. When no reds remain on the table, player's on balls become the colors, in ascending numerical order (2, 3, 4, 5, 6, 7). These legally pocketed colors are not spotted after each is pocketed; they remain off the table (the seven-ball is an exception in the case of a tie score: see "Scoring").

ILLEGALLY POCKETED BALL: Reds illegally pocketed are not spotted; they remain off the table. Colors illegally pocketed are spotted (see "Spotting Balls").

JUMPED OBJECT BALLS: Reds jumped off the table are not spotted; no penalty. Colors jumped off the table are spotted; no penalty.

SPOTTING BALLS: Reds are never spotted. Colors to be spotted are placed as at the start of the game. If a color's spot is occupied (to mean that to spot it would make it touch a ball), it is placed on the spot of the highest value color that is unoccupied. If all spots are occupied, the color is spotted as close as possible to its original spot on a straight line between its spot and the nearest point on the foot cushion.

CUE BALL AFTER JUMP OR SCRATCH: Incoming player has cue ball in hand within the D. When cue ball is in hand within the D (except on the opening break), there is no restriction (based on position of reds or colors) as to what balls may be played; player may play at an on ball regardless of where it is on the table.

PENALTY FOR FOULS: Seven points are added to non-fouling player's score for each foul committed (no deduction from offender's score). Incoming (non-offending) player has the choice of either (1) accepting the table in position and shooting, or (2) requiring the offending player shoot again; if the foul is a cue ball jump off the table or a cue ball scratch, the cue ball is in hand within the D for either player. If the foul is other than cue ball jump off the table or scratch, the cue ball remains in position.

GENERAL RULES OF CAROM BILLIARDS

The rules in this section apply generally to all the specific forms and varieties of carom billiard games included in this rulebook. Certain games, however, do have exceptions that supercede and/or modify the General Rules; these exceptions are flagged with a parenthetical notation, referencing the particular game or variation in which the general rule might be either modified or nonapplicable. Thus, unless specifically noted otherwise, these General Rules apply to all carom billiard games.

To facilitate the use and understanding of these General Rules, many terms that may require definition for some readers are set in italic in their first appearance, so that the reader may refer to the **Glossary of Billiard Terms** section for the exact meaning of the term.

For purposes of simplicity and clarity, masculine pronouns have been utilized throughout this rulebook. Obviously, such references should be considered to apply to any player, regardless of gender.

Although most references in these rules are to a "player" or "players;" since most carom billiard games can be adapted to team play, the reader should interpret the rules as equally applicable to a team of teams when appropriate.

The United States Billiard Association today sanctions most U.S. play of the popular carom game of **Three-Cushion Billiards.** In the individual game rules for Three-Cushion, the U.S.B.A. official rules have been reprinted exactly as published by that group, resulting in some duplication of General Rules from this section within U.S. B. A.'s rules.

TABLES, BALL, EQUIPMENT. All games are contested on tables, and with balls and equipment, meeting the standards prescribed in the **BCA Specifications.**

The Carom Table

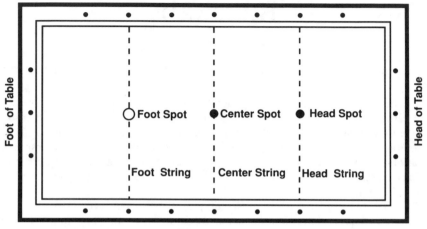

Diagram No. 12

BALLS DEFINED. Two white balls and a red; each player has a white ball that is a cue ball when he is shooting, while the red is never a cue ball. One of the white balls has two or three small colored spots to differentiate it from the other. (**Note: Four Ball** is played with a fourth ball as well; see **Four Ball** rules.)

STRIKING CUE BALL. Legal shots require that the *cue ball* only be stuck with the *cue tip* only.

DETERMINING FIRST PLAYER. The player to perform the *opening break* shot is determined by either *lag for break* or *lot.* (The lag-for-break procedure is required for formal competition.) The player winning the lag or lot has the choice of performing the opening break shot or assigning it to the opposition.

LAG FOR BREAK. Red ball is spotted on *foot spot* (except in *Four Ball*). With the *cue balls in hand behind the head string,* one player to the right and one to the left of the *head spot,* the balls are shot to the foot *cushion* and back to the head end of the table. The player whose ball ends up closest to the head cushion wins the lag, subject to the following qualifications:

The lagged ball must contact the foot cushion at least once; other cushion contacts are immaterial except as prohibited below. It is an automatic loss of the lag if (1) the ball crosses into the opponent's half of the table, or (2) the ball fails to contact the foot cushion, or (3) the ball jumps the table, or (4) the ball hits the red ball.

If both players violate automatic-loss lag rules as above, or if the referee is unable to determine which ball is closer, the lag is a tie and is replayed.

The lag for opening break is performed by both players simultaneously, although they need not stroke the lag shots in perfect unison.

CHOICE OF CUE BALLS. The winner of the lag has the choice of cue balls, either the all-white "clear" or the color-marked "spot," which is then used throughout the game. If an odd number of players are competing, the same cue ball is **not** played throughout the game. Rather, incoming player always plays the cue ball that was **not** used by the player who immediately preceded him (Exception: **Four Ball Caroms**).

BALL POSITIONS – OPENING BREAK. The red ball is spotted on the foot spot. Non-breaking player's cue ball is spotted on the *head spot*. Breaking player's cue ball is placed on the *head string* within six inches (measured to the ball's center) of the head spot. (Note: **Four Ball** uses a different opening break position.)

The Break Shot

Diagram No. 13

RED BALL FIRST OBJECT. Player making opening break shot must contact the red ball first, rather than the opponent's cue ball. If the cue ball on the opening break strikes the other white ball first rather than the red ball, it is an *error* and ends his *inning*; no score is valid. (Exception: **Four Ball Caroms**.)

On all subsequent shots, players may make either the red or the white (or "pink" in **Four Ball**) ball his first object (first ball struck by the cue ball). (Exception: **Red Ball**.)

FOOT ON FLOOR. It is a foul if a player shoots when at least one foot is not in contact with the floor. Foot attire must be normal in regard to size, shape and the manner in which it is worn.

SHOOTING WITH BALLS IN MOTION. It is a foul if a player shoots while the cue ball or any object ball is in motion. (A spinning ball is in motion.)

COMPLETION OF STROKE. A stroke is not (complete and therefore is not counted) until all balls on the table have become motionless after the stroke. (A spinning ball is in motion.)

FOULS BY TOUCHING BALLS. It is a foul to strike, touch or in any way make contact with the cue ball in player or any object balls in play with anything (the body, clothing, chalk, *mechanical bridge, cue shaft*,etc.) **except** the cue tip (while attached to the cue shaft), which may contact the cue ball once in the execution of a shot.

FOULS BY DOUBLE HITS. It is a foul if the cue ball is struck more than once on a shot by the cue tip. If, in the referee's judgement, the cue ball has left initial contact with the cue tip and then is struck a second time in the course of the same stroke, it shall be a foul. If the referee judges, by virtue of sound, ball position and action, and stroke used, that there were two separate contacts of the cue ball by the cue tip on a stroke, the stroke is a foul and must be so-called.

PUSH SHOT FOULS. It is a foul if the cue ball is pushed or shoved by the cue tip, with contact being maintained for more than the momentary time necessary for a stroked shot. If the referee judges that the player put the cue tip against the cue ball and then pushed or shoved on into the shot, maintaining contact beyond the normal momentary split-second, the stroke is a foul and must be so-called.

JUMPED CUE BALL. When a stroke results in the cue ball being a *jumped ball,* the stroke is a foul. (Note: jumped object balls may or may not be fouls; see specific game rules.)

GENERAL RULE, ALL FOULS. Though the penalties for fouls differ from game to game, the following applies to all fouls: (1) player's inning ends, and (2) if on a stroke, the stroke is invalid and cannot be a scoring stroke.

ILLEGAL JUMPING OF BALL. It is a foul if a player strikes the cue ball below center ("digs under" it) and **intentionally** causes it to rise off the bed of the table (usually in an effort to clear an obstructing ball). Such jumping action may occur accidentally on occasion, and such "jumps" are not necessarily considered fouls; they may still be ruled foul strokes however, if for example, the ferrule or cue shaft makes contact with the cue ball in the course of the shot.

SPECIAL INTENTIONAL FOUL PENALTY. The cue ball in play shall not be **intentionally** struck with anything other than a cue's attached tip (such as the ferrule, shaft, etc.). While such contact is automatically a foul under the provisions of "Fouls By Touching Balls," if the referee deems the contact to be intentional, he shall warn the player **once** during a match that a second violation during that match will result in the loss of the match by forfeiture, If a second violation does occur, the match must be forfeited.

BALLS MOVING SPONTANEOUSLY. If a ball shifts, settles, turns or otherwise moves "by itself," the ball shall remain in the position it assumed and play continues.

PLAYER RESPONSIBILITY FOULS. The player is responsible for chalk, bridges, files and any other items or equipment he brings to, uses at, or causes to approximate the table. If he drops a pen or a piece of chalk, or knocks off a mechanical bridge head, as examples, he is guilty of a foul should such an object make contact with a ball in play.

JUMPED BALLS DEFINED. Balls coming to rest other than on the bed *of the table* after a stroke (on the cushion top, rail surface, floor, etc.) are considered jumped balls. Balls may bounce on the cushion tops, rails or light fixtures of the table in play without being jumped balls **if** they return to the bed of the table under their own power and without touching anything not a part of the table equipment. The table equipment shall consist of its light fixture, and any permanent parts of the table proper. (Balls that strike or touch anything not a part of the table equipment shall be considered jumped balls even though they might return to the bed of the table after contact with the non-equipment item[s]).

All jumped balls are spotted when all balls have stopped moving. (See "Spotting Jumped Balls.")

OUTSIDE INTERFERENCE. If the balls are moved (or a player bumped such that play is directly affected) by a non-player during a match, the balls shall be replaced as near as possible to their original positions immediately prior to the incident, and play shall resume with no penalty on the player affected. If the match is officiated, the referee shall replace the balls. This rule shall also apply to "act of God" interference, such as earthquake, hurricane, light fixture falling, a power failure, etc.

DEFINITION OF LEGAL SAFETY. Player must drive an object ball to a cushion or cause the cue ball to contact a cushion after striking an object ball. Failure to do so is a foul. (Note: U.S.B.A. Three-Cushion rules prohibit all **intentional** safeties.)

LIMIT ON SAFETY PLAY. Player may not play safety in consecutive innings. When a player's last shot was a safety, he must not play another safety on his next shot. If he does so, it is a foul. (Note: does not apply in U.S.B.A. Three-Cushion play.)

PLAYING FROM SAFETY. When a player has either fouled or played an intentional safety on his last shot, he comes to the table for his next shot "playing from safety."

Player must make an obvious and legal attempt to score. If he again resorts to safety play, whether or not the effort meets the requirements of a legal safety, he has fouled. (Note: "Playing From Safety" does not apply in Three-Cushion.)

SPOTTING JUMPED BALLS. If the cue ball is jumped off the table (foul), it is spotted on the head spot (if occupied, the foot spot; if that is also occupied; the center spot).

If the white object ball is jumped, it is spotted on the head spot (if occupied, the foot spot; if that is also occupied, the center spot).

If the red object ball is jumped, it is spotted on the foot spot (if occupied, the head spot; if that is also occupied, the center spot). If the cue ball and an object ball are both jumped, the cue ball is spotted first, then the object ball following the appropriate spotting order above.

If both object balls are jumped, they are spotted as above. If the cue ball occupies either of the object balls' primary spot locations, spot first the ball that spots freely; then the other according to the appropriate alternative spotting order above.

(A spotting location is "occupied" if a ball cannot be placed on that spot without contact occuring.)

If all three balls are jumped, they are spotted as for the opening break.

When the cue ball is not jumped, any score made on a shot when a ball is jumped is valid and the player continues his inning after spotting the object ball(s); no penalty.

(Note: Three-Cushion rules differ in spotting and scoring; also Foul Ball differs.)

KISS SHOTS. All kiss shots are fair, and need not not be called, whether they deprive a player of an imminent score, or whether they assist in a score.

SHOOTING WRONG CUE BALL. If a player shoots with the wrong cue ball and the error is detected and called before the stroke is complete, it is a foul. (**Note:** U.S.B.A. rules differ – see Rule #8.)

If a player shoots the wrong cue ball and the error is undetected until after the stroke is complete, it is not a foul, but it does end the offending player's inning. Any *count* or counts scored previous to the error's detection are credited to the shooter.

(Example: player runs two with the wrong ball, but when he shoots for the third count, opponent [or referee] detects the error and calls it **before** the stroke is complete. Disposition: first two counts are good, last stroke is foul; player scores a net score of two for the inning.) **Note:** U.S.B.A. rules differ.

(Example: player runs three with the wrong ball, with the error being detected and called by the opponent [or referee] **after** the third stroke is complete. Disposition: the run of three counts is good, though player's inning ends; player gets a score of three for the inning.) **Note:** U.S.B.A. rules differ.

In all cases after wrong cue ball calls, incoming player accepts the table in position.

The referee will **not** warn a player who is about to shoot with the wrong ball, but will call the stroke foul immediately upon its execution. **Note:** U.S.B.A. rules differ.

If an opponent's cue ball is shot in error and is jumped off the table on the stroke, it is a foul and the ball shall be spotted according to the rules for spotting opponent's cue ball (assuming, of course, that the error is detected prior to the next shot).

COMPLETION OF STROKE. A stroke is not complete (and therefore is not counted) until all balls on the table have become motionless after the stroke. (A spinning ball is in motion.)

FROZEN BALLS. If the cue ball is frozen to an object ball, shooting player has two choices: (1) have the frozen balls (ONLY) spotted (red on foot spot, player's cue ball on head spot, opponent's cue ball on center spot), or (2) play them as they lie with the restriction that the cue ball must be "shot away from" the ball(s) to which it is frozen (i.e., the cue ball must contact a cushion or an unfrozen ball before it contacts the frozen ball(s); failure to successfully "shoot away from" the frozen ball(s) is a foul.

If choice #1 is made and the appropriate spot for a ball to be spotted is occupied by another ball, the ball to be spotted is placed on the spot appropriate to the occupying (interfering) ball. (A spotting location is "occupied" if a ball cannot be placed on that spot without contact occuring.)

CUE BALL FROZEN AGAINST CUSHION. When the cue ball is *frozen* to a cushion, it may be played against that cushion first, but that impact does not count as a cushion if specific game rules require cushion play. (If the cue ball contacts the same cushion a second time, that impact counts, as do all succeeding impacts, if any, on the same cushion.)

COUNT ON CUSHION DEFINED. When specific game rules require cushion play of one or more cushions, a cushion contact shall mean an impact of the cue ball with a cushion (**except** as restricted in the special situation when cue ball is frozen to a cushion – see "Cue Ball Frozen Against Cushion"). The number of valid cushions contacted does not necessarily mean that number of different cushions of the table; more than one valid cushion impact may be accomplished on the same table cushion, if the impacts are distinct and separate as a result of overspin or underspin on the cue ball.

If the cue ball bounces and rides on top of the cushion or rail and returns to the bed of the table (within the perimeters of "Jumped Balls Defined"), each cushion or rail it rides shall count as one cushion only, regardless of how many actual bounces or impacts of the cue ball might occur.

——— BANK BILLIARDS ———

Except when clearly contradicted by these additional rules,
the **General Rules of Carom Billiards** apply.

PLAYERS: 2 or 3.

BALLS USED: Standard set of one white, one white spot and one red.

OBJECT OF THE GAME: Score the predetermined number of points (usually 60 in tournament play, or any agreed upon number) for game prior to opponent(s).

SCORING: Each legal *count* is scored as one point for shooter.

DEFINITION OF A COUNT: A shot is a count if not in violation of any "Rules of Play" or **General Rules of Carom Billiards**, and the *cue ball* contacts both object balls.

RULES OF PLAY:

1. A legal counting stroke entitles shooter to continue at the table until he fails to legally count on a shot.

CUSHION CAROMS

Except when clearly contradicted by these additional rules,
the **General Rules of Carom Billiards** apply.

PLAYERS: 2 or 3.

BALLS USED: Standard set of one white clear, one white spot, and one red.

OBJECT OF THE GAME: Score the predetermined number of points (may be 30-60 in tournament play, or any agreed upon number) for game prior to opponent(s).

SCORING: Each legal *count* is scored as one point for shooter.

DEFINITION OF A COUNT: A shot is a count if not in violation of any "Rules of Play" or **General Rules of Carom Billiards**, and the cue ball contacts both object balls.

OPENING BREAK: General Rules of Carom Billiards regarding opening break apply, as well as "Rule of Play" #2 below. Failure to comply is a violation; player's *inning* ends and no count can be scored.

RULES OF PLAY:

1. A legal counting stroke entitles shooter to continue at the table until he fails to legally count on a shot.

2. On all shots, player must cause the cue ball to either (1) contact one or more cushions before contacting object balls, or (2) contact an object ball directly and then one or more cushions before it contacts second object ball. Failure to comply is a violation; player's inning ends and no count can be scored on the violating stroke.

PENALTY FOR FOULS: One point is deducted from offender's score for each *foul*.

FOUR BALL CAROMS

Except when clearly contradicted by these additional rules,
the **General Rules of Carom Billiards** apply.

PLAYERS: 2.

BALLS USED: Standard set of one white clear, one white spot and one red, plus one light red (pink).

OBJECT OF THE GAME: Score the predetermined number of points for game prior to opponent.

SCORING: Each legal two-ball *carom* count is scored as one point for shooter; each legal three-ball carom count is scored as two points for shooter.

DEFINITION OF A COUNT: If not in violation of any "Rules of Play" or **General Rules of Carom Billiards**, a shot is: a two-ball carom *count* if the *cue ball* contacts any two of the three object balls, or a three-ball carom count if the cue ball contacts all three of the object balls.

BALL POSITIONS – OPENING BREAK: The light red (pink) ball is *spotted* on the *foot spot*. The red ball is spotted on the *head spot*. Both balls are in position before the *lag for break*.

OPENING BREAK: The lag for break is actually part of the *opening break* with the red and pink balls spotted as immediately above, players select cue balls and lag for break as in **General Rules of Carom Billiards** (automatic loss of lag applying to contact with the pink ball as well as the red). When lag is completed, both players' cue balls remain in position; first shot of the game is from this position (if cue ball[s] contacted wither red and/or pink object balls – which were spotted – on lag, they are respotted prior to first shot of game). Winner of lag has choice of shooting first or assigning first shot to opponent; in either case, cue balls are played from position following lag for break, and each player's cue ball is the one he used for the lag for break. Starting player (first shooter after lag for break) must cause the cue ball's first contact with a ball to be with the pink object ball (on the foot spot). Failure to comply is a violation; player's inning ends and no count can be scored.

RULES OF PLAY:

1. On all shots subsequent to the first shot following the lag, shooter may make his first object (first balls contacted by the cue ball) any of the three object balls.

2. A legal counting stroke entitles shooter to continue at the table until he fails to legally count on a shot.

SPOTTING JUMPED BALLS: (Differs from **General Rules of Carom Billiards**)

If the red ball is jumped off the table, it is spotted on the *head spot*. If the head spot is occupied (spotting a ball on it would result in contact with another ball), the red ball is held off the table until the first time the head spot is vacant at the completion of a shot.

If the pink ball is jumped, it is spotted on the foot spot. If the foot spot is occupied (spotting a ball on it would result in contact with another ball), the pink ball is held off the table until the first time the foot spot is vacant at the completion of a shot.

If the white object ball is jumped, it is spotted on the head spot. If the head spot is occupied, the white object ball is held off the table until the first time the head spot is vacant at the completion of a shot. Should the head spot be occupied after each shot until such time as the white object ball is required as incoming player's cue ball, that ball shall then be spotted on the foot spot; if the foot spot is also occupied, it shall be spotted on the center spot; if the center spot is also occupied, incoming player may place the ball anywhere on the head string, not *frozen* to a ball.

If the white cue ball is jumped, the same rule (immediately above) applies.

If the red ball and the pink balls are jumped on a shot, spot the pink ball first, then the red ball, according to spotting rules for those balls. If neither can be spotted per those rules, spot the pink ball on the center spot and continue holding the red ball off the table until the head spot is vacant per the red spotting ball rule.

If either one of the white balls and one or both of the red balls are jumped on a shot, first spot the white ball per appropriate rule above, then the red ball per appropriate rule (or if both reds, the immediately preceding paragraph).

If both of the white balls and one of the red balls is jumped, spot all balls that will spot directly (beginning with the white object ball, then the white cue ball, then the red). If all jumped balls cannot be spotted directly, spot remaining balls per appropriate rule above.

If all four balls are jumped on a shot, the jumper's cue ball is spotted on the center spot, the red ball on the head spot, the pink on the foot spot, and the incoming player may place his cue ball anywhere on the head string not frozen to the red ball.

Jumped balls result in no penalty unless the player's cue ball is jumped. If player does jump his cue ball off the table, the stroke is invalid and is a foul.

PENALTY FOR FOULS: One point is deducted from offender's score for each foul.

———— RED BALL ————

Except when clearly contradicted by these additional rules,
the **General Rules of Carom Billiards** apply.

PLAYERS: 2 or 3.

BALLS USED: Standard set of one white clear, one white spot and one red.

OBJECT OF THE GAME: Score the predetermined number of points for game prior to opponent(s).

SCORING: Each legal *count* is scored as one point for shooter.

DEFINITION OF A COUNT: A shot is a count if not in violation of any "Rules of Play" or **General Rules of Carom Billiards** and the *cue ball* contacts both object balls.

OPENING BREAK: General Rules of Carom Billiards regarding *opening break* apply. Failure to comply is a violation; player's inning ends and no count can be scored.

RULES OF PLAY:

1. A legal counting stroke entitles shooter to continue at the table until he fails to legally count on a shot.

2. On all shots, player must make his first object (first ball contacted by the cue ball) the red ball. Failure to do so is a foul.

PENALTY FOR FOULS: One point is deducted from offender's score for each *foul*.

———— STRAIGHT RAIL ————

Except when clearly contradicted by these additional rules,
the **General Rules of Carom Billiards** apply.

PLAYERS: 2 or 3.

BALLS USED: Standard set of one white clear, one white spot and one red.

OBJECT OF THE GAME: Score the predetermined number of points for game prior to opponent(s).

SCORING: Each legal *count* is scored as one point for shooter.

DEFINITION OF A COUNT: A shot is a count if not in violation of any "Rules of Play" or **General Rules of Carom Billiards** and the *cue ball*, contacts both object balls.

OPENING BREAK: General Rules of Carom Billiards regarding *opening break* apply. Failure to comply is a violation; player's inning ends and no count can be scored

RULES OF PLAY:

A legal counting stroke entitles shooter to continue at the table until he fails to legally count on a shot.

2. When the object balls are in a *crotch*, player may score no more than three successive counts with the balls remaining in the crotch. If three successive in-crotch counts are made, player must, on his next shot, drive at least one object ball out of the crotch. Failure to do so is a violation; players's inning ends and no count can be scored.

PENALTY FOR FOULS: One point is deducted from offender's score for each foul.

—— THREE-CUSHION BILLIARDS ——

Except when clearly contradicted by these additional rules,
the **General Rules of Carom Billiards** apply.

PLAYERS: 2 or 3.

BALLS USED: Standard set of one white clear, one white spot, and one red.

OBJECT OF THE GAME: Score the predetermined number of points (usually 30-60 in tournament play, or any agreed upon number) for game prior to opponent(s).

SCORING: Each legal *count* is scored as one point for shooter.

DEFINITION OF A COUNT: A shot is a count if not in violation of any "Rules of Play" or **General Rules of Carom Billiards**, and the cue ball either:

1. contacts an object ball and then contacts three or more *cushions*, and then strikes the other object ball; or,

2. contacts three or more cushions, and then contacts the two object balls; or,

3. contacts a cushion and then an object ball, then two or more cushions and then the other object ball; or,

4. contacts two or more cushions and then an object ball, then one or more cushions and then the other object ball.

OPENING BREAK: **General Rules of Carom Billiards** regarding *opening break* apply. Failure to comply is a violation; player's *inning* ends and no count can be scored.

RULES OF PLAY:

1. A legal counting stroke entitles shooter to continue at the table until he fails to legally count on a shot.

2. If a player causes any ball to jump off the table, the shot is a *foul*. (Balls are spotted as in **General Rules of Carom Billiards.**)

3. In playing a deliberate *safety* by contacting an object ball that is *frozen* to a cushion, the cushion on which the object ball is frozen is valid for **General Rules of Carom Billiards**. "Frozen Ball," rule only for the *cue ball*, even if more than one impact of the frozen ball is caused. If the cue ball does not contact a cushion on such a shot, the attempt at safety is a foul unless the object ball is driven to contact a different cushion. (The rules regarding safety play are not to be construed as apply to *mis-cues* or mis-hits that are the result of apparent honest intent to score; such shots shall not be ruled foul even though they may fail to fulfill rules for safeties.)

PENALTIES FOR FOULS: Player's inning ends and the stroke cannot be a count (no point penalty or deduction).

—— UNITED STATES BILLIARD ——
ASSOCIATION
THREE-CUSHION RULES

1. USBA sanctioned tournaments will be governed by the rules that follow. Any exception must be stated in the tournament notice, or discussed and approved by a majority of the players present before the start of any USBA tournament.

2. A three-cushion billiard is valid and is a count of one in any of the following cases: a) cue ball strikes an object ball and then strikes three or more cushions before striking the second object ball; b) cue ball strikes three or more cushions and then strikes the two object balls; c) cue ball strikes a cushion, then strikes one object ball, and then strikes two or more cushions before striking the second object ball; d) cue ball strikes two cushions, then strikes first object ball, and then strikes one or more cushions before striking the second object ball.

3. Three cushions means three impacts. The number of cushions does not mean three different ones; a valid count may be executed on one cushion, if they are the result of the overspin or underspin on the ball.

4. Lagging for the Break. a) The two players select a cue ball, which is placed on the table within the head string, and stroke the ball to the foot of the table and return. The side rails may be touched by the ball in lagging, though it is not required. b) Player whose ball comes to rest nearest to the head rail wins the lag. c) The winner of the lag has the right to shoot the first shot or assign the break shot to the opponent. d) Winner of the lag has the choice of cue balls, which is then used for the duration of the game.

5. Break Shot. a) Opponent's ball is placed on the head spot. Starting player's cue ball is placed within eight inches to the right or left of the head spot. Red ball is placed on the foot spot. b) Starting player must contact red ball first. Failure to contact red ball first is an error and ends the starting player's inning. c) On subsequent shots, either red ball or cue ball can be the first object ball.

6. Fouls Which End a Player's Turn. a) Jumped balls (see Rule 11). b) Starting play while balls are in motion. c) Touching any of the balls by hand, part of clothing, cue or any other object such as chalk or pen. The balls shall remain in position to which they were thus moved. d) Push or shove shot (see Rule 15). e) Double stroke (see Rule 15). f) When, at moment of shooting, neither foot is touching the floor. g) Wrong ball (see Rule 8). h) Touching ball with cue during warm-up (see Rule 18). i) Player interference (see Rule 20).

7. Any foul caused by outside interference is not to be charged as a penalty to the player with shot in progress. If the balls are displaced by the disturbance, they will be restored to their original position as precisely as possible, and the player will continue shooting.

8. Wrong Ball. a) Shooting with the wrong ball is a foul and ends the player's inning. b) The opponent or the referee may call this foul; opponent may call before or after the shot, referee calls it only after the shot. c) Such a foul can be called at any time during a run, but the shooter shall be entitled to all points made

previous to the stroke in which error was detected. d) The incoming shooter shall play the balls as left after error was called.

9. Frozen Balls. a) If during the course of an inning the shooter's ball comes to rest in contact with the opponent's ball, the shooter has the option of playing away from the ball with which he is in contact, or elect to have the balls in contact spotted. b) If an inning ends with the shooter's ball in contact with the next shooter's ball, or the red ball in contact with the next shooter's ball, the incoming player has the option of playing away from the ball in contact, or may elect to have the two balls which are in contact spotted. c) Only those balls which are in contact are to be spotted. The loose or unfrozen ball is not to be touched. The red ball is spotted on the foot spot, the player's cue ball on the head spot, and the opponent's cue ball on the center spot. d) If the spot reserved for the ball to be spotted is hidden by another ball, the ball to be spotted is placed on the spot usually reserved for the hiding ball. e) The same rules apply when a ball or balls jump the table.

10. When a cue ball is frozen to a cushion, a player may shoot into (play against) that cushion, but the first contact shall not count. Subsequent contacts with the same cushion are valid.

11. When a player's cue ball, the opponent's ball, or the red ball jumps the table, it is a foul and the player's inning ends. Spot balls as per Rule #9 (c,d).

12. No shot can be started while balls are still in motion, or are still spinning. If a player disregards this rule, it is a foul and inning ends.

13. When the cue ball bounces and rides the top of the rail and returns to the table, the ball is in play. It shall count as one cushion. If it rides two or more rails, each rail will count as a cushion. If ball remains on top of the rail, it is considered a jumped ball, which is a foul, and player's inning ends.

14. If in playing a shot the cue ball leaves the playing surface and rides the rail or cushion, regardless of the number of impacts on that cushion, only one impact will be allowed.

15. If a player has pushed or shoved the cue ball with his cue, it is a foul and player's inning ends. A push shot is one in which the cue tip remains in contact with the cue ball after cue ball strikes an object ball, or when cue tip again contacts the cue ball after cue ball strikes the object ball. Double stroke is similar and occurs when player's trip or cue shaft hits cue ball twice. If a billiard is made, it shall not count, and the player's inning ends.

16. All kiss shots are fair, whether they deprive a player of an imminent score, or whether they assist in a score.

17. Miscues shall not end the player's inning, unless it is construed that the player's ferrule or shaft also touched the cue ball. Not all miscues are fouls, and if a billiard is completed in the miscue stroke, it shall be counted and turn continues.

18. If a player during the "warm-up" stroking should touch the cue ball, it is a foul and inning ends.

19. A game is official when a player scores the number of points designated as constituting a game, even though the opponent has had one less turn at the table. If a scorekeeper is used, the game becomes official after the score sheet is signed

by the players. The referee and the scorekeeper should also sign the sheet. After the losing player signs the score sheet, no protest can be made.

20. If a player at the table is responsible for interference in any manner, it is a foul, and the inning ends. Incoming player must accept balls in position. A player not at the table must not distract the opponent with undue motions or noise. The referee or tournament official may issue a warning or disqualify the player for unsportsmanlike conduct.

21. If, for reasons beyond his control, a player cannot start a game as scheduled, the game may be postponed if the tournament director so decides. If a player is unable to finish a game, he forfeits the game, unless the opponent waives the forfeiture and agrees to finish the game at a time convenient to the tournament management. If a player is unable to return to the tournament, all his games are nullified as they would be in disqualification.

2. If a player is disqualified in a game, he loses that game and gets no points. The opponent is credited with a game won and is given the number of points he would have scored had he won the game. If a player is disqualified from a tournament, all his games are nullified (that is, games played and games remaining on the schedule). Tournament continues as though one less player started when tournament opened.

23. If, for reasons beyond his control, a player cannot start a game, he must notify the tournament manager in time to allow for a substitute player, or for another pair of players. All tournament contestants are subject to immediate call if a substitute is necessary.

24. If a referee is officiating and considers a player to be taking an abnormal amount of time between strokes or in determining the choice of shots with the intention of upsetting his opponent, the referee shall warn the player that he runs the risk of disqualification if he pursues these tactics. Continued disregard of the warning shall be proper grounds to disqualify the player. If no referee is officiating, the tournament manager shall have the right to invoke this rule.

25. Deliberate safeties are not allowed. If played, the incoming player may accept balls as they are, or set up a break shot.

26. At any tournament sanctioned by the USBA, the tournament director plus some other member of the USBA who is not playing in the tournament shall constitute a grievance committee to whom unsportsmanlike conduct during the tournament may be reported. Before commencement of the tournament, the players shall designate two of the players to serve on such a committee to protect the interests of the players. The two persons representing the USBA and the two persons representing the players shall jointly consider any evidence or reports of unsportsmanlike conduct. If this grievance committee is unable to resolve the complaint, the representatives shall submit a written report to the USBA for consideration by the Board of Directors. The two player representatives may indicate their concurrence in the findings of the USBA representatives or may submit dissenting views to the Board of Directors. At the next regular meeting or special meeting of the Board of Directors, these reports shall be considered and the action recommended by a majority shall be binding on the accused membe of the USBA.

THE DIAMOND SYSTEM

There are various systems in billiards which allow a player to figure out his angles by simple arithmetic. The most common of these is the diamond system.

Billiard players argue as to the value of systems, some claiming they are not essential to good billiard play. On the other hand, champion players, who know the angles as well as anyone, use the diamond system to check their "instinct." Many players attain Class A skill without knowledge of the diamond system, but the indisputable fact remains that it takes all guesswork out of 3-cushion billiards.

The diamond system is based on a knowledge of connecting diamonds. The player must memorize the connecting diamonds. See Diagram. Note that the cushions are designated first, second, third and fourth cushions. On the third cushion, the diamonds are marked 1,2,3,4,5,6,7 and 8 (the latter being the corner). The same diamond markings are on the first cushion.

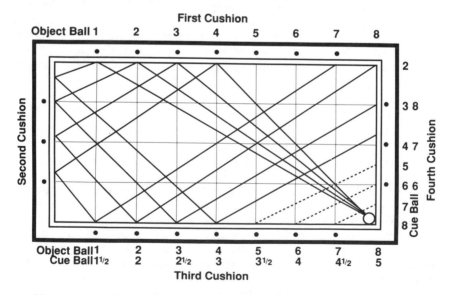

Now, a cue ball hit with slight running English that strikes the third rail at diamond No. 1 will travel back to diamond No. 7 on the first cushion. If it strikes diamond No. 2 on the third rail it will travel back to diamond No. 8 on the first rail (or corner). Diamond No. 3 on the third rail connects with diamond No. 3

112

(object ball number) on the lower rail. The various diamonds connect as illustrated in the diagram. A player must memorize these connections to use the diamond system, since he must know the path the ball will travel after it comes off the third rail.

Playing the diamond system the player studies his shot backwards–that is, he must find out where he will come off the third cushion to score. Say, for example, that both object balls lie in the corner at the first cushion and lower rail. That would be the lower right hand corner on the diagram. (See illustration)

The player, having memorized the connecting diamonds, knows that he must come off diamond No. 2 on the third rail to bank the shot in that corner.

Now, note that there are object ball markings on the third cushion. They start from No. 1 at the first diamond and go down to 8 which is the corner. If the player has to come off the second diamond, his object ball number is 2.

Now, note there are cue ball numbers on the third cushion. They start with 1-$\frac{1}{2}$ on the first diamond and go down to 5, which is the corner. The cue ball numbers also continue on the lower rail, as 6, 1$\frac{1}{2}$, 7, and 8. (See diagram.)

The player is still playing the bank shot with the two object balls in the lower right hand corner. He knows up to this time that he must come off diamond No. 2 on the third rail to count.

Now, he must figure out where he will hit on the first cushion to bring his cue ball back to diamond No. 2 on the third cushion. In the diagram the cue ball lies at cue ball No. 5, which is the corner. Thus, knowing the object ball number (2) and the cue ball number (5), he subtracts the object ball number (2) from the cue ball number (5) and gets 3, which is the diamond he must hit on the first rail. If he wants to get to diamond No. 1 on the third rail, with the cue ball still at 5, he subtracts 1 from 5 and gets 4, the diamond he must hit on the first rail. If he wants to get to 3 on the third rail, he subtracts 3 from 5 and gets 2.

If he wants to get 2 on the third rail and finds the cue ball is at 6 on the lower rail, he subtracts 2 from 6 and gets 4 which is where he will hit on the first rail. If the cue ball lies at 3-$\frac{1}{2}$ as a cue ball number and he wants to get to 2 on the third rail, he subtracts 2 from 3-$\frac{1}{2}$ and gets 1-$\frac{1}{2}$, which he must hit on the first rail.

Now, note that when a ball lies at cue ball position No. 5 (see diagram) and the player is playing to come off the cushion at 2 on the third rail, player must hit 3 on the first cushion. The diagram shows a line running from cue ball position 5 to the 3 diamond on the first cushion.

That line is cue ball position 5, no matter where the cue ball rests on that line. If the ball is in the corner it is 5. If the cue ball is on the line and four inches from the first cushion, it is still cue ball number 5.

Our discussion to this point covered only bank shots. Now, we want to make a 3-cushion carom shot, driving the cue ball from the first object ball into three cushions and thence to the second object ball. In shots of this type, the first object ball gives the player his cue ball number. Suppose the first object ball lies on the line of cue ball position 5 we discussed immediately above. If the player drove the object ball on cue ball line 5 into the first cushion at diamond No. 3, he would hit the third cushion at 2 and travel to the lower right hand corner; assuming the second object ball is in that corner.

However, the player cannot drive the object ball with his cue. So–knowing the first object ball rests on cue ball line 5, he must drive the cue ball from the first object ball into the first cushion at diamond No. 3 to come off the third rail at diamond No. 2 and make the shot on the second object ball in the lower right hand corner. Here, the ability to make caroms reveals its importance.

The most important thing in 3-cushion billiards is being able to drive the cue ball from the first object ball into the first cushion at the point desired. In other words, unless the player can make the simple carom of driving the cue ball from the first object ball into the desired point of the first cushion, his chances of making the count are minimized.

If the first object ball lies on cue ball track (or line) 4-$\frac{1}{2}$ and the player wants to come off diamond No. 2 on the third cushion, he subtracts 2 from 4-$\frac{1}{2}$ and then proceeds to drive his cue ball off the first object ball into 2-$\frac{1}{2}$ on the first cushion (which is 2 from 4-$\frac{1}{2}$).

Many players refuse to learn the diamond system, because written explanations of it are somewhat complicated and require studious attention. However, if the player will follow the instructions above and test them out on a table, he will find the system is comparatively simple. Oral explanations from a player who knows the system make for easier understanding, of course.

The diamond system is not infallible, but on bank shots particularly it serves a player better than his instinct. If you watch a player in world's tournaments as he studies a bank shot, he will determine first from what point he must come off the third rail to score.

Say he has to come off diamond 2-$\frac{1}{2}$ on the third rail. He then determines his cue ball number. Say it is 4-$\frac{1}{2}$. By subtracting 2-$\frac{1}{2}$ from 4-$\frac{1}{2}$ he knows he must hit diamond No. 2 on the first rail to get back to diamond No. 2-$\frac{1}{2}$ on the third rail.

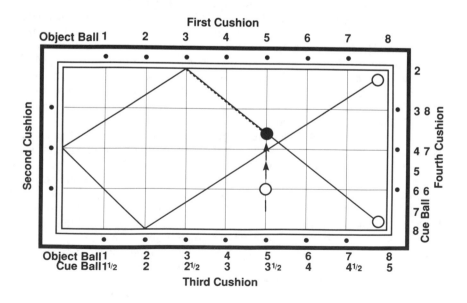

The system tells him exactly where to hit. His instinct may have given him the general location of the desired point on the first cushion, but if he hit 1-³/₄ or 2-¹/₄ on the first rail, chances are he would miss the shot.

When using the diamond system, strike the cue ball in the center with slight running English, following through on your stroke. If you stab the cue ball with a jerky stroke you will shorten the angle. If you slam the cue ball too hard you are likely to shorten the angle. Use a stroke of medium force and follow through.

If the balls do not lie exactly on the object ball and cue ball tracks, you may parallel or you may figure the diamonds in fractions. For example, if the object ball number is 1-¹/₄ and the cue ball number is 3-¹/₂, your subtraction gives you point 2-¹/₄ on the first rail. The diamond system does not apply to all shots on the table. It is confined almost entirely to natural angle shots.

You may find that in using the diamond system on a certain table that your cue ball "comes short." If this happens, you allow for it in your calculations, moving up higher on the first rail. Thus, instead of hitting 2 (assuming your calculations tell you to hit 2) you move up to 1-³/₄ or maybe 1-¹/₂. Make sure first, however, that you are stroking your cue ball with running English and are following through before you decide the table runs "short."

When using the diamond system, aim at the diamond through the cushion–that is, at an angle through the cushion to the diamond, which is set back on the rail. Do not aim at a point at the edge of the cushion which is directly opposite the diamond.

THREE-CUSHION PRACTICE SHOTS

Object Ball	1	2	3	4	5	6	7	8
Cue Ball	1½	2	2½	3	3½	4	4½	5

No. 1 Three Cushion Shot

Hold cue level. Hit object ball 1/3 right. Strike cue ball cemter, slight english left. Use 7 inch bridge. Employ moderate stroke.

Object Ball	1	2	3	4	5	6	7	8
Cue Ball	1½	2	2½	3	3½	4	4½	5

No. 2 Three or Four Cushion Shot

Hold cue level. Hit object ball 1/4 left. Strike cue ball center, english left. Use 6 inch bridge. Employ moderate stroke.

No. 3 Three or Four Cushion Shot

Hold cue level. Hit object ball 1/4 left. Strike cue ball center, english right. Use 7 inch bridge. Employ moderate stroke.

No. 4 Five or Six Cushion Shot

Hold cue level. Hit object ball thin. Strike cue ball center, english right. Use 8 inch bridge. Employ hard stroke.

BCA HALL OF FAME

The purpose of the Hall of Fame is to honor outstanding persons of the world who, through their competitive skills and/or dedication, have enriched the game of billiards.

Two categories have been established in BCA's Hall of Fame. The **Greatest Players** category will consist of players who have been active in national competition for at least 15 years and have won at least one recognized national championship. At least one candidate from this category will be nominated annually. The **Meritorious Service** category is reserved for persons who have made lasting, memorable and important contributions to billiards, even though they may not have distinguished themselves as competitors.

Pictured on the following pages are those who have the distinct honor of membership in the BCA Hall of Fame.

Ralph Greenleaf
inducted 1966

Fourteen-time World Pocket Billiard Champion, RALPH GREENLEAF, possessed all the flash and flair of a natural showman. With his beautiful actress wife, Princess Nai Tai Tai, the handsome Greenleaf put together a sparkling trick-shot performance and toured the vaudeville circuit in the 20s and 30s.

The audiences watched him perform his spectacular shots by looking at a huge mirror suspended on stage over the playing table.

Greenleaf won his first Pocket Billiard championship in 1919 and his last one in 1937.

William F. Hoppe
inducted 1966

WILLIE HOPPE, whose brilliant career was one of the longest in the annals of the sport, is considered by many to be the greatest all-around billiard player of any era.

In 1906, at the tender age of 18, Hoppe won his first world's title by defeating the renowned French champion, Maurice Vignaux, at 18.1 Balkline in a memorable match in Paris. He went on to win the 18.2 Balkline and Cushion Carom titles and years later, between 1936 and 1952, held the Three-Cushion title 11 times.

Charles C. Peterson
inducted 1966

CHARLIE PETERSON earned the title "Missionary of Billiards" for his untiring efforts to promote the game throughout the United States.

In addition to being the world's fancy-shot champion and, for years, holder of the Red Ball title, Peterson made scores of personal appearances at colleges and universities across the country and was the guiding spirit of the Intercollegiate and Boys' Clubs of America tournaments.

Peterson died in 1962 at the age of 83, after a life devoted to winning friends for the sport of billiards.

Welker Cochran
inducted 1967

WELKER COCHRAN, a champion who trained for his billiard matches with the same intensity as a professional boxer, won his first of two 18.2 Balkline titles in 1927. He later went on to become the Three-Cushion champion five times in the 30s and 40s.

Like many stars of the sport, Cochran learned the game in his father's billiard establishment, and he became the protege of Frank Gotch, the wrestler, who sent young Cochran to Chicago to hone his playing talents.

Alfredo DeOro
inducted 1967

The career of the distinguished Spanish champion, ALFREDO DeORO, encompassed both Three-Cushion and Pocket Billiards and spanned the closing decades of the 19th century and the opening decades of the 20th.

DeOro, who served in his country's diplomatic corps, first gained the Pocket Billiard crown in 1887. He was to repeat the achievement 16 times in the next 25 years. DeOro held the Three-Cushion title 10 times from 1908 through 1919.

In 1934, at the age of 71, DeOro came out of retirement for a Championship Tournament, winning two dramatic victories from defending champion Welker Cochran and the ultimate winner of the tournament, Johnny Layton.

Benjamin B. Nartzik
inducted 1967

BEN NARTZIK will always be remembered for his tireless crusade to revive billiards from its severe doldrums in the 1950s. Nartzik deserves a lion's share of the credit for ridding the game of its "pool hall" image and re-establishing its status as a "gentleman's sport." Under his leadership, the BCA was able to help both the Boys Club of America and the Association of College Unions to organize billiard programs and run successful annual tournaments. Nartzik recognized the potential of the industry and bought the National Billiard Chalk Co. of Chicago.

**Willie Mosconi
inducted 1968**

For most people, the name WILLIE MOSCONI and the sport of Pocket Billiards are synonymous. And rightly so, since from 1940 to 1957 Mosconi had a near-stranglehold on the World Title, winning it 15 times in that period. Born in Philadelphia in 1913, Willie was a prodigy with the cue by the age of seven. At 20, he embarked on a hectic cross-country exhibition tour with his idol, Ralph Greenleaf, then World Champ and at the height of his game. The result, 57 wins for Greenleaf, an amazing 50 wins for the young Mosconi. One of the most astounding of Mosconi's many records is his yet-unbroken exhibition high run of 526 balls!

**Jake Schaefer, Sr.
inducted 1968**

"A player whose super-brilliance with a billiard cue won for him the sobriquet of 'Wizard'..." so runs the lead of a 1909 newspaper article singing the praises of JAKE SCHAEFER, SR. From the last quarter of the 19th century through the first decade of the 20th, Schaefer, Sr. was one of the most feared names in Balkline Billiards. Derivations of the game were invented just to stymie his genius – all unsuccessfully. He traveled throughout the world winning matches and gathering fans. On March 11, 1908, though desperately ill, he successfully defended his title in his final match for the 18.1 championship against Willie Hoppe by a score of 500 to 423.

**Jake Schaefer, Jr.
inducted 1968**

Billiard historians generally rank JAKE SCHAEFER, JR. as the greatest of the American Balkline players. He was the world champion at 18.2 in 1921, 1925, 1926, 1927, and 1929-1933. He held the 18.1 honors in 1926-1927 and the 28.2 title in 1937-1938. At the 18.2 game, he holds four records which have never been equalled in this country: best game average, 400 (from the break); grand average, tournament, 57.14; grand average, match, 93.25; high run, match, 432.

**Herman J. Rambow
inducted 1969**

Called the Stradivari of his trade by those who know, HERMAN RAMBOW crafted custom cues for the greatest players in billiards over the course of a 65-year career. Captains of industry and celebrities of the entertainment world also beat a path to his door to have the privilege of paying from $50 to $300 for one of his perfectly-balanced "Rambow Specials." It was Herman who perfected the jointed cue by inserting a countersunk screw in the recessed butt end, making an extra-sturdy connection. Only death at age 86 stopped the craftsman from his labor of love. To billiard cognoscenti the world over, there will never be another Rambow.

**Harold Worst
inducted 1970**

HAROLD WORST of Grand Rapids, Michigan was only 19 years old when he played the great Willie Hoppe, winner of 51 major billiard championships, in a demonstration game in Detroit in 1949. Hoppe soon took an interest in Worst's playing potential, and under his guidance, Worst won the world title for three-cushion billiards in Argentina in 1954, the youngest player to compete in world competition. He successfully defended this title for many years.

**John Wesley Hyatt
inducted 1971**

JOHN WESLEY HYATT, known as the father of the American plastic industry, was an inventor rather than a player, but his invention of the celluloid plastic billiard ball in 1868 revolutionized the billiard industry. Hyatt began his search for a suitable synthetic billiard ball material when a New York billiards firm offered a $10,000 prize for a substitute for ivory. Hyatt's earlier attempts involved shellacking a paper pulp sphere and a ball made of layers of cloth.

**Frank Taberski
inducted 1975**

FRANK TABERSKI was born in 1889 and grew up in Schenectady, N.Y. At the age of 26, he attended a pocket billiard championship in New York City, and came home convinced he played as well as the champions. The next year, he entered and placed third behind Johnny Layton. From then on, he was almost invincible. In those days, 450 point challenge matches were the means of competition; the prize a ruby and diamond studded gold medal with the proviso that any one who won 10 consecutive challenge matches could keep it. Alfredo DeOro had come closest with five straight defenses. By 1918 Taberski had accomplished the impossible and the medal was his.

**Johnny Layton
inducted 1976**

JOHNNY LAYTON, born in Sedalia, Mo., in 1891, won the world's three-cushion championship 12 times, defeating such champions as Willie Hoppe, Welker Cochran, Jake Schaefer, Jr. and Augie Kieckhefer in the 20s and 30s. Layton recorded the high three-cushion game mark of 50 points in 23 innings, a record which still stands today. He was credited with originating the method of using the diamond system, using table markers to indicate direction of ball rebounds, a style that he perfected through the application of his highly developed mathematical mind.

**James Caras
inducted 1977**

JIMMY CARAS was born in 1910 in Scranton, Pennsylvania, and is the second living person to be elected the Hall of Fame. Jimmy started playing billiards at the age of five. When seventeen, he defeated Ralph Greenleaf in an exhibition match to become known as the Boy Wonder of The World . Nine years later, in 1936, he won his first world championship. He won again in 1938, 1939 and in 1949. Eighteen years later, in 1967, he won the U.S. Open in a field of 48 players. His record of "most balls", "most games won" and "fewest innings by a champion" still stand in the record book for that size field.

**Irving Crane
inducted 1978**

IRVING CRANE was born in 1913 in Livonia, New York. His love for the game started as a child, when he was given a toy billiard table. Although he played steadily as a teenager, he did not enter tournament play until the age of twenty-three. He won his first world title in 1942. Since then, he has won almost two dozen major championships, including the world crown in 1946, 1955, 1966, 1968, 1970, 1972, plus the International Roundrobin championship in 1968.

Crane was the victor in the 1978 World Series of Billiards (a combination of 14.1 and 9-ball) against a strong field of outstanding competitors. His greatest triumph, however, was his victory in the 1966 U.S. Open, when he won the championship in a never-to-be-excelled record run of 150-and out.

**Steve Mizerak
inducted 1980**

STEVE MIZERAK, born September 12, 1944 in Perth Amboy, New Jersey, was the youngest inductee to the BCA Hall of Fame. In the brief span of his career, he has been 4 times champion of the U.S. Open, winning the title in 1970, 1971, 1972, and 1973. Mizerak also captured the PPPA World Open title in 1982 and 83. He won two World Pocket Billiards titles in 1983 and 1984. Mizerak continues to finish near the top in several national tournaments each year.

**Dorothy Wise
inducted 1981**

DOROTHY WISE was born in Spokane, Washington on December 13, 1914. In her early years, there were very few national tournaments for women. Since she was in many local and state tournaments, she became the self-proclaimed world champion. When BCA staged the first national tournament for women in 1967, she immediately entered. For the next 5 years, she proved herself most worthy as she won 5 consecutive U.S. Open titles.

Joseph Balsis
inducted 1982

JOE BALSIS was born in Minnersville, Pa., on June 23, 1921. Balsis never could resist knocking the balls around one of the pool tables at father John Balsis' recreation room. By the time he was 11, Balsis was playing exhibitions against the likes of Andrew Ponzi and Erwin Rudolph. He won junior titles four consecutive years. During pool's doldrum years Balsis left the game and it wasn't until 1944 that Balsis, a boat machinist in the Coast Guard, won his next title; Armed Services Champ. In '64 "the Meatman," as Balsis is known because of his family's meat business, returned to competi tive pool. Between 1965 and 1975 Balsis competed in the finals of the U.S. Open five times, winning twice ('68 & '74). He won the prestigious Billiard Room Proprietor's Association tournament in '65, then captured the World All-Around championship in Johnston City, Ill., in 1966. He won the Jansco brothers' Stardust Open all-around title back-to-back in '68 and '69.

Luther Lassiter
inducted 1983

Considered by many to be the finest 9-ball player ever, LUTHER LASSITER was born in 1919 in Elizabeth City, NC. Lassiter earned his nickname "Wimpy," for all the hot dogs and Orange Crushes he could pack away as a youngster hanging around the local pool hall. By the time he was 17, "Wimpy" was packing away his share of opponents. Lassiter's biggest years in tournament play came in the '60s. In the eleven years of the Jansco brothers' all-around championships in Johnston City, Ill. (1962-72), Lassiter won the straight pool title five times, the nine-ball title four times and the one-pocket title once. On three occasions Lassiter went on to capture the All-Around title ('62, '63, '67). He also won the BCA U.S. Open in '67 and the Stardust World All-Around championship in '71.

"Minnesota Fats"
inducted 1984

Perhaps the most recognizable figure in the history of pool, RUDOLPH "Minnesota Fats" WANDERONE was elected to the Hall of Fame for "Meritorious Service." Although he never actually won a designated "world championship" Wanderone, the game's leading comic, orator and publicity generator, has probably done more for the game in terms of sheer exposure than any other player. Initially nicknamed "Brooklyn Fats," and "New York Fats," Wanderone dubbed himself "Minnesota Fats" after the film version of "The Hustler" hit movie screens around the country in the early 1960's. Since that time he has become known around the world as pool's foremost side show.

"Fats," whose exact age is a mystery, hosted a national television show, "Celebrity Billiards," during the '60s. He stopped playing in tournaments all together around that time.

Jean Balukas
inducted 1985

JEAN BALUKAS is the second woman inducted into the BCA Hall of Fame. She was born in 1959 in Brooklyn, New York, making her the Hall's youngest member. An excellent all-around athlete, Jean competed in her first BCA U.S. Open when she was 9 years old, finishing seventh. She won her first BCA crown when she was 12. Since then Jean has collected seven BCA U.S. Open 14.1 titles, six World Open titles and countless 9-ball and straight pool crowns. She has been named Player of the Year five times.

Lou Butera
inducted 1986

LOU BUTERA was born in Pittston, Pennsylvania in 1938. He learned to play at his father's pool room in the small coal-mining town. After watching BCA Hall of Famer Erwin Rudolph in an exhibition, 14-year-old Lou decided to devote his life to pool. He was runner-up to Irving Crane in the 1972 World Championship in Los Angeles. In 1973 he defeated Crane in the finals of the same event to win his first World Championship. Nicknamed "Machine Gun Lou" for his rapidfire style, Lou recorded a 150-ballrun against Allen Hopkins in just 21 minutes in 1973. Butera has since won numerous titles.

Erwin Rudolph
inducted 1987

ERWIN RUDOLPH was born December 31, 1894, in Cleveland. Rudolph did not participate in his first world 14.1 championship until he was 24 years old. Five years later, in 1926, Rudolph gained national acclaim by ending Ralph Greenleaf's six-year reign as world champion. Rudolph's win over Greenleaf came in a challenge match. After losing his world title to Thomas Huesten, Rudolph regained the crown by winning the 1933 world championship. He won his third world title in 1933, and, at age 47, captured his fourth and final world crown by defeating a young Irving Crane in the finals of the 1941 world championship in Philadelphia. At the time of his death in 1957, he held the record for fastest game in a world tournament, scoring 125 points in just 32 minutes. (The record has since been eclipsed.)

Andrew Ponzi
inducted 1988

ANDREW PONZI was born Andrew D'Allesandro in 1903 in Philadelphia. He acquired the name Ponzi after a witness to his cue prowess compared the likelihood of beating D'Allesandro with beating the infamous "Ponzi Scheme," an early version of the pyramid game. A dazzling offensive player, Ponzi competed in the game's Golden Era, the '30s and '40s, against the likes of Mosconi, Crane, Caras, Rudolph and Greenleaf. Despite that stiff competition, Ponzi captured World 14.1 titles in 1934, '40 and '43. Ponzi died in Philadelphia in 1950.

Michael Sigel
inducted 1989

MIKE SIGEL, at 35, became the youngest male elected to the BCA Hall of Fame. Born in Rochester, NY, in 1953, Sigel began playing pool at 13, and turned professional when he was 20. A natural right-hander who shoots left-handed, Sigel won his first major tournament, the U.S. Open 9-Ball Championship, in 1975. His career blossomed quickly, and Sigel was perhaps the game's dominant player in the 1980s. He amassed 38 major 14.1 and 9-ball championships in that decade. Sigel has won three World 14.1 crowns (1979, '81 and '85) and one World 9-Ball title (1985) as well as numerous national titles.

John Brunswick
inducted 1990

JOHN BRUNSWICK, born in 1819, was a Swiss immigrant woodworker who founded what has become the Brunswick Corporation, the largest pool table manufacturer in this country. Producing his first billiard table in 1845, Brunswick went on to develop an American market for billiard equipment. He is credited with the rapid growth of billiards in the late 19th century.

TOURNAMENT RESULTS
AND RECORDS

For records of tournaments no longer held, check the listings at the back of this section first and then prior editions of the BCA Official Rules and Record Book.

BCA NATIONAL INDIVIDUAL 8-BALL CHAMPIONS

Men's Division

1977–Tom Kilburn, Dayton, OH, ...Runner-up–Dick Spitzer
1978–Mike Carella, Louisville, KY, ...Runner-up–Bob Williams
1979–Jimmy Reid, Louisviile, KY, ...Runner-up–Mark Wilson
1980–Nick Varner, Columbus, OH, ...Runner-up–Mike Massey
1981–Danny Diliberto, Las Vegas, NV, ...Runner-up–Nick Varner
1982–Joe Sposit, Kansas City, MO, ...Runner-up–Gregg Fix
1983–Michael Sardelli, Detroit, MI, ...Runner-up–Tom Chapman
1984–Louie Lemke, Fort Worth, TX, ...Runner-up–Charles Shotman
1985–Steve Matlock, Cedar Rapids, IA, ...Runner-up–Stan Fimple
1986–Jesus Rivera, CO, ...Runner-up–Mickey Leon Stone
1987–Stan Fimple, Omaha, NE, ...Runner-up–Mike Fenne
1988–Harry Sexton, Detroit, MI, ...Runner-up–Seco Varani
1989–Henry Granas, Englewood, CO, ...Runner-up–T.J. Davis
1990–Jesus Rivera, Denver, CO ....Runner-Up–Gilbert Martinez

Women's Division

1978–Catherine Stephens, Louisville, KY, ...Runner-up–Melodie Horn
1979–Gloria Walker, Louisville, KY, ...Runner-up–Mary Kenniston
1980–Billie Billings, Columbus, OH, ...Runner-up–Gloria Walker
1981–Belinda Campos, Las Vegas, NV, ...Runner-up–Sherry Lively
1982–Linda Hoffman, Kansas City, MO, ...Runner-up–Sherry Lively
1983–Georgina Casteel, Detroit, MI, ...Runner-up–Sherry Lively
1984–Belinda Campos Bearden, Fort Worth, TX, ...Runner-up–Linda Hoffman
1985–Linda Hoffman, Arlington, TX, ...Runner-up–Diane Piercy
1986–Linda Hoffman, Arlington, TX, ...Runner-up–Christine Glass
1987–Linda Hoffman, Arlington, TX, ...Runner-up–Janene Hague
1988–Timi Bloomberg, Rapid City, SD, ...Runner-up–Kathy Miao
1989–Sherry Lively, Carmichael, CA, ...Runner-up–Christine Glass
1990–Linda Meyer, Ponca City, OK ....Runner-Up–Janene Hague

Senior Men's Division

1986–Stanley Coscia, Tampa, FL, ...Runner-up–Harold Schnormeier
1987–Jerry Priest, Cape Girardeau, MO, ...Runner-up–Bob Keating
1988–Seco Varani, Faribault, MN, ...Runner-up–Bob Keating
1989–Jerry Priest, Cape Girardeau, MO, ...Runner-up–Bob Vanover
1990–Jerry Priest, Cape Girardeau, MO ....Runner-Up–Bernard Rogoff

1989–Fern Reedy, Smithville, MO, ... Runner-up–Jeanne Bloomberg
1990–Jeri Engh, Osceola, WI .... Runner-Up–Op Wheeler

BCA ALL-AMERICAN 8-BALL TEAM CHAMPIONS

Women

1979 .... Wheel Inn (Billings, MT)
1980 .... Burt's Girls (Colorado Springs, CO)
1981 .... Burt's Girls (Colorado Springs, CO)
1982 .... Richard's (Lansing, MI)
1983 .... Richard's (Lansing, MI)
1984 .... North Star (Sacramento, CA)
1985 .... Gold Nugget (Arlington, TX)
1986 .... Leisure Club (Phoenix, AZ)
1987 .... Leftys + (Sacramento, CA)
1988 . Great American Girls (Sacramento, CA)
1989 .... 8-Ball Express (Rapid City, SD)
1990 .... 8-Ball Express (Rapid City, SD)

Men

1979 . Tam O'Shanter (Colorado Springs, CO)
1980 . Tam O'Shanter (Colorado Springs, CO)
1981 . Tam O'Shanter (Colorado Springs, CO)
1982 ...... The Wizards (Colorado Springs, CO)
1983 .... Mike's Lounge (Pittsburgh, PA)
1984 .... Green Acres (Ft. Worth, TX)
1985 .... Starlite Lounge (Arlington, TX)
1986 .... MeMaws (Ft. Worth, TX)
1987 ..... Jackson All Stars (Grand Prairie, TX)
1988 ... Mongo Murph's (Windsor, CANADA)
1989 .... Black Sticks (Houston, TX)
1990 .... Black Sticks (Houston, TX)

BCA NATIONAL JUNIOR 8-BALL CHAMPIONS

1989–Chan Whitt, Jr., Lewisburg, WV, ... Runner-up–Chad Duster
1990–Nathan Haddad, Lansing, MI (15-18 division) .... Runner-up–Scott Marshall
   –Michael Coltrain, Raleigh, NC (14 and under) .... Runner-up–Chris Whitten

BCA SANCTIONED TOURNAMENTS

LONE STAR 8-BALL TOURNAMENT, AMARILLO, TX

1. Henry Chavez   2. Mike Giles   3. Benny Edwards   4. Tony Beard

4th ANNUAL ALASKA STATE STRAIGHT POOL CHAMPIONSHIP, ANCHORAGE, AK

1. Robert Colby   2. Buddha Hiramoto   3. Al Bryan   4. Flapper Hamilton

WINTERFEST POOL TOURNEY, BUFFALO, NY

1. Barry McQuillen   2. Joseph Wojciechowski   3. Rick Bauza   4. Rick Sees

SNOOKERS OCEAN STATE 9-BALL CHAMPIONSHIP, PROVIDENCE, RI

1. Rick Marcos   2. Bob Cross   3. Mark Ranson   4. Bruce DiFronzo

SHOOTING STARS POOL TOURNEY, BUFFALO, NY

1. Joe Wojciechowski   2. Barry McQuillen   3. Santo   4. Jerry Ravenzahn

*STRIPES & SOLIDS 8-BALL TOURNAMENT, PUERTO RICO
*CAN-AM POOL TOURNEY, BUFFALO, NY
*THRILLA FOR THE GORILLA, BUFFALO, NY
*ON THE SNAP POOL TOURNEY, AMHERST, NY
*J.D. STOKES 8-BALL TOURNAMENT, STONERIDGE, NY
*MINT BAR OPEN, PLAINS, MT
*HAMILTON PARK INVITATIONAL, FLORHAM PARK, NJ
*BENEFIT TOURNAMENT FOR DISABLED VIETNAM VETERANS, KENMORE, NY

* No tournament results available.

ACU-I POCKET BILLIARD CHAMPIONS (Men)

1937	John O. Miller	University of Wisconsin
1938	J. L. Geiger	University of Florida
1939	Peter Choulas	Colgate University
1940	John O. Miller	University of Wisconsin
1941	Lloyd Green	University of Kansas
1942	Leo Bonimi	Cornell University
1943	L. Mabie	University of Florida
1944	J. Zvanya	University of Indiana
1945-46	(No Tournament)	
1947	Leff Mabie	University of Florida
1948	Jack Brown	University of Utah
1949	Leroy Kinman	Eastern Kentucky State
1950	Leroy Kinman	Eastern Kentucky State
1951	Leroy Kinman	Eastern Kentucky State
1952	Bill Simms	University of Georgia
1953	John Beaudette	Michigan State College
1954	John Beaudette	Michigan State College
1955	Rodney Boyd	Ohio State University
1956	Joseph Sapanaro	Suffolk University
1957	Joseph Sapanaro	Suffolk University
1958	Lloyd Courter	State University of Iowa
1959	Donald Dull	State College of Washington
1960	Henry Parks	Indiana University
1961	Jim Finucane	University of Notre Dame
1962	Robert Burke	University of Oregon
1963	Larry Galloway	Indiana University
1964	William Hendricks	Southern Illinois University
1965	William Wells	Tulane University
1966	William Wells	Tulane University
1967	Richard Baumgarth	Purdue University
1968	Marshall Boelter	Univ. of Illinois, Chicago Circle Campus
1969	Nick Varner	Purdue University
1970	Nick Varner	Purdue University
1971	Keith Woestehoff	Ohio University
1972	Andrew Tennent	University of Wisconsin
1973	Dan Louie	Washington State University
1974	Dan Louie	Washington State University
1975	Robert Jewett	University of California–Berkeley
1976	John Cianflone	Rutgers University
1977	Jay Hungerford	Arizona State University
1978	Steve Cusick	University of Illinois–Urbana
1979	Peter Lhotka	University of North Dakota
1980	Rob Havick	University of Minnesota–Duluth
1981	(No Tournament)	
1982	Thomas Golly	Penn State University
1983	Robert Madenjian	Kansas State University
1984	Gary French	California State College–Stanislaus
1985	(No Tournament)	
1986	Gary Asbell	Florida State University
1987	Bill Beardsley	University of Michigan
1988	Nick Kucharew	Mohawk College
1989	Gary Asbell	Florida State University
1990	Marc Oelslager	St. Cloud State University

ACU-I POCKET BILLIARD CHAMPIONS (Women)

1929 .... Margaret Anderson .... University of Illinois
1942 .... Emily Ann Julian .... South Dakota State College
1943 .... Mary Jean Noonan .... South Dakota State College
1944 .... Barbara Jackson .... Colorado State College of Ed.
1948 .... Jeanne Lynch .... Rhode Island State
1949 .... Cora Libbey .... University of Wisconsin
1950 .... (No Tournament)
1951 .... Ramona Fielder .... South Dakota State College
1952 .... Sondra Bilsky .... Purdue University
1953 .... Joanne Skonning .... Purdue University
.... Jackie Slusher .... Oregon State College
1954 .... Lee McGary .... University of Oregon
1955 .... Judy Ferles .... University of Arizona
1956 .... Judy Ferles .... University of Arizona
1957 .... No Co-ed Face to Face ....
1958 .... No Co-ed Face to Face ....
1959 .... Jan Deeter .... Purdue University
1960 .... Darlene McCabe .... University of Oregon
1961 .... Ann Sidlauskas .... Indiana University
1962 .... San Merrick .... Bowling Green State University
1963 .... Barbara Watkins .... Bowling Green State University
1964 .... Barbara Watkins .... Bowling Green State University
1965 .... Susan Sloan .... University of Texas
1966 .... Linda Randolph .... Iowa State University
1967 .... Shirley Glicen .... University of Miami
1968 .... Gail Allums .... University of Iowa
1969 .... Donna Ries .... University of Missouri at Kansas City
1970 .... Catherine Stephens .... Western Washington State
1971 .... Marcia Girolamo .... State Univ. of New York at Oswego
1972 .... Krista Hartmann .... Santa Fe Junior College, Gainsville, Florida
1973 .... Marcia Girolamo .... State University of New York at Oswego
1974 .... Janice Ogawa .... Boise State University
1975 .... Debra Weiner .... Northern Illinois University
1976 .... Melissa Rice .... University of Wisconsin–Milwaukee
1977 .... Julie Bentz .... University of Wisconsin–Madison
1978 .... Mari Dana Heydon .... Oregon State University
1979 .... Julie Bentz Fitzpatrick .... University of Wisconsin–Madison
1980 .... Shari Verrill .... University of Wisconsin–Madison
1981 .... (No Tournament)
1982 .... Jane Bartram .... University of Colorado
1983 .... Helen Yamasaki .... California State University–LA
1984 .... Shirley Weathers .... Triton College
1985 .... (No Tournament)
1986 .... Kathy Trabue .... Ohio State University
1987 .... Penny Beile .... University of Kentucky
1988 .... Janet Dordell .... Penn State University
1989 .... Cathy Petrowski .... North Texas State University
1990 .... Susan Tillotson .... Florida State University

BCA'S U.S. OPEN 14.1 POCKET BILLIARD CHAMPIONSHIP RECORDS

Men's Division

Irving Crane 1966, Chicago, IL .... Runner-up–Joe Balsis
Jimmy Caras 1967, St. Louis, MO .... Runner-up–Luther Lassiter
Joe Balsis 1968, Lansing, MI .... Runner-up–Danny DiLiberto
Luther Lassiter 1969, Las Vegas, NV .... Runner-up–Jack Breit
Steve Mizerak 1970, Chicago, IL .... Runner-up–Luther Lassiter
Steve Mizerak 1971, Chicago, IL .... Runner-up–Joe Balsis
Steve Mizerak 1972, Chicago, IL .... Runner-up–Dan DiLiberto
Steve Mizerak 1973, Chicago, IL .... Runner-up–Luther Lassiter
Joe Balsis 1974, Chicago, IL .... Runner-up–Jim Rempe
Dallas West 1975, Chicago, IL .... Runner-up–Pete Margo
Tom Jennings 1976, Chicago, IL .... Runner-up–Joe Balsis
Tom Jennings 1977, Dayton, OH .... Runner-up–Richard Lane
Dallas West 1983, Detroit, MI .... Runner-up–Nick Varner
Oliver Ortmann 1989, Chicago, IL .... Runner-up–Steve Mizerak

Women's Division

Dorothy Wise 1967, St. Louis, MO .... Runner-up–San Lynn Merrick
Dorothy Wise 1968, Lansing, MI .... Runner-up–San Lynn Merrick
Dorothy Wise 1969, Las Vegas, NV .... Runner-up–San Lynn Merrick
Dorothy Wise 1970, Chicago, IL .... Runner-up–Shelia Bohm
Dorothy Wise 1971, Chicago, IL .... Runner-up–Geraldine Titcomb
Jean Balukas 1972, Chicago, IL .... Runner-up–Madelyn Whitlow
Jean Balukas 1973, Chicago, IL .... Runner-up–Donna Ries
Jean Balukas 1974, Chicago, IL .... Runner-up–Mieko Harada
Jean Balukas 1975, Chicago, IL .... Runner-up–Mieko Harada
Jean Balukas 1976, Chicago, IL .... Runner-up–Gloria Walker
Jean Balukas 1977, Dayton, OH .... Runner-up–Gloria Walker
Jean Balukas 1983, Detroit, MI .... Runner-up–Loree Jon Ogonowski
Loree Jon Jones 1989, Chicago, IL .... Runner-up–Robin Bell

U.S. OPEN RECORDS – 1966-1977
Men's Division

High run in the money: 150 by Irving Crane (vs. Joe Balsis), 1966.

High run out of the money: 116 by Rodney "Babe" Thompson, 1972.

High BPI average, tournament: 18.66 by Steve Mizerak, 1972.

High BPI average, career (minimum 3 Opens or 10 games): 12.47 by Steve Mizerak.

High BPG average, tournament: 158.3 by Dallas West, 1975.

High BPG average, career (minimum 3 Opens or 10 games): 136.3 by Steve Mizerak.

Most balls, tournament (48-man field): 1788 by Jimmy Caras, 1967.

Most balls, tournament (32-man field): 1319 by Luther Lassiter, 1970.

*Most balls, tournament (16-man field): 1235 by Tom Jennings, 1977.

*Most balls, career: 10,026 by Joe Balsis (1966-1977 inclusive).

Most games, tournament (48-man field): 12 by Jimmy Caras, 1967.

Most games, tournament (32-man field): 10 by Luther Lassiter, 1970.

*Most games, tournament (16-man field): 8 by Tom Jennings, 1977.

*Most games, career: 77 by Joe Balsis (1966-1977 inclusive).

*Fewest innings by champion (16-man field): 165 by Tom Jennings, 1977.

Most championships won: 4 by Steve Mizerak; 1970-1973 inclusive.

Most consecutive championships won: 4 by Steve Mizerak, 1970-1973 inclusive.

Most runner-up finishes: 3 by Balsis (1966, 1971, 1976) and Lassiter (1967, 1970, 1973).

Most third place finishes: 2 by Mizerak (1969, 1975) and West (1973, 1976).

Greatest victory margin (150-point match): 163 by Dick Baertsch (vs. Balsis), 1969.

Most innings, tournament (54-man field): 214 by Norman Webber, 1968.

Most innings, tournament (32-man field): 168 by Irving Crane, 1975.

*Most innings, tournament (16-man field): 165 by Tom Jennings, 1977.

*Most innings, career: 983 by Dallas West (1966-1977 inclusive).

Most games won, tournament (48-man field): 11 by Jimmy Caras, 1967.

Most games won, tournament (32-man field): 8 by Luther Lassiter, 1970.

*Most games won, tournament (16-man field): 7 by Tom Jennings, 1977.

* Most games won, career: 55 by Joe Balsis (1966-1977 inclusive).

Best winning percentage, tournament: 1,000 by Crane, 1966; Mizerak, 1971; West, 1975.

Best winning percentage, career (minimum 3 Opens or 10 games): .792 by Steve Mizerak.

Fewest innings by champion (54-man field): 134 by Joe Balsis, 1968.

Fewest innings by champion (48-man field): 162 by Jimmy Caras, 1967.

Fewest innings by champion (32-man field): 53 by Steve Mizerak, 1972.

Most consecutive match victories: 12 by Steve Mizerak (1970-1972).

Most high run awards: 3 by West (1966, 1967, 1976) and Balsis (1968, 1969, 1973).

Best game (150 points): 1 inning by Irving Crane (vs. Balsis), 1966.

Best game (200 points): 16 innings by Joe Balsis (vs. J. Rempe), 1974.

*Most appearances, career: 12 by Joe Balsis and Dallas West (1966-1977 inclusive).

*Most money won, career: $27,625 by Joe Balsis.

* New records in 1977.

U.S. OPEN RECORDS – 1967-1977
Women's Division

*High run in the money: 51 by Jean Balukas (vs. Vicki Frechen), 1977.

High run out of the money: 28 by Jean Ann (Williams) Cardwell, 1967.

*High BPI average, tournament: 4.71 by Jean Balukas, 1977.

*High BPI average, career (minimum 3 Opens or 10 games): 2.51 by Jean Balukas.

*High BPG average, tournament: 81.25 by Jean Balukas, 1977.

*High BPG average, career (minimum 3 Opens or 10 games): 73.6 by Jean Balukas.

Most balls, tournament (16-woman field): 546 by Mieko Harada, 1974.

Most balls, tournament (12-woman field): 429 by San Lynn Merrick, 1967.

Most balls, tournament (8-woman field): 398 by Gerry Titcomb, 1969.

Most balls, career: 3583 by Gerry Titcomb.

Most games, tournament (16-woman field): 8 by Madelyn Whitlow, 1972.

Most games, tournament (8-woman field): 6 by Gerry Titcomb, 1969, 1971.

Most games, career: 55 by Gerry Titcomb.

Most innings, tournament (16-woman field): 373 by Madelyn Whitlow, 1972.

Most innings, tournament (12-woman field): 274 by Gerry Titcomb, 1967.

Most innings, tournament (8-woman field): 219 by Gerry Titcomb, 1970.

Most innings, career: 1958 by Gerry Titcomb.

Most games won, tournament (16-woman field): 6 by Madelyn Whitlow, 1972.

Most games won, tournament (12-woman field): 5 by Jean Balukas (1976) and Dorothy Wise (1967).

Most games won, tournament (8-woman field): 4 by several players.

*Most games won, career: 35 by *Jean Balukas and Gerry Titcomb.

Best winning percentage, tournament: 1,000 by Wise (67-68, 70-71) and Balukas (72-77).

*Best winning percentage, career (minimum 3 Opens or 10 games): .854 by Jean Balukas.

Fewest innings by champion (16-woman field): 113 by Jean Balukas, 1975.

Fewest innings by champion (12-woman field): 109 by Jean Balukas, 1976.

*Fewest innings by champion (8-woman field): 69 by Jean Balukas, 1977.

*Most championships won: 6 by Jean Balukas; 1972-1977 inclusive.

*Most consecutive championships won: 6 by Jean Balukas; 1972-1977 inclusive.

Most runner-up finishes: 2 by San Lynn Merrick, Gerry Titcomb and Mieko Harada.

Most third place finishes: 5 by Gerry Titcomb 1970, 1972, 1974, 1975, 1976.

*Most consecutive match victories: 29 by Balukas (1972-1977 inclusive).

*Most high run awards: 4 by *Balukas (72, 73, 75, 77) and Wise (67, 68, 70, 71).
*Best game (75 points): 3 innings by Jean Balukas (vs. Belinda Campos), 1977.
*Best game (100 points): 19 innings by Jean Balukas (vs. Gloria Walker), 1977.
  Most appearances, career: 10 by Gerry Titcomb (1967-1976 inclusive).
*Most money won, career: $12,800 by Jean Balukas.

* New records in 1977.

BILLIARD FEDERATION OF U.S.A. CHAMPIONS

1968 .... Allen Gilbert	1979 .... Eddie Robin
1969 .... Bill Hynes	1980 .... Harry Sims
1970 .... Allen Gilbert	1981 .... George Ashby
1971 .... Allen Gilbert	1982 .... Carlos Hallon
1972 .... Eddie Robin	1983 .... Harry Sims
1973 .... John Bonner	1984 .... George Ashby
1974 .... Frank Torres	1985 .... Frank Torres
1975 .... John Bonner	1986 .... Carlos Hallon (held in March '86)
1976 .... George Ashby	1987 .... Allen Gilbert
1977 .... Allen Gilbert	1988 .... Allen Gilbert
1978 .... Frank Torres	

AMERICAN BILLIARDS ASSOCIATION

1969 .... Bud Harris	1984 .... Carlos Hallon .... Eastern
1970 .... Bud Harris	.... George Ashby .... Central
1971 .... Jim Cattrano	.... not held .... Western
1972 .... Jim Cattrano	1985 .... 3 tied for 1st .... Eastern
1973 .... Allen Gilbert	Ira Goldberg
1974 .... not held	Bill Maloney
1975 .... George Ashby	Dick Reid
1976 .... Allen Gilbert	.... George Ashby .... Central
1977 .... Allen Gilbert	.... Rick Bryck .... Western
1978 .... George Ashby	1986 .... Dick Reid .... Eastern
1979 .... George Ashby	.... Bill Smith .... Central
1980 .... George Ashby	.... Nahib Yousri .... Western
changed to 3 Regionals	1987 .... Dick Reid .... Eastern
1981 .... Carlos Hallon .... Eastern	.... George Ashby .... Central
.... George Ashby .... Central	.... Harry Sims .... Western
.... Allen Gilbert .... Western	1988 .... Carols Hallon .... Eastern
1982 .... Chris Bartzos .... Eastern	.... Mike Donnelly ...... Central
.... Bill Hawkins .... Central	.... Allen Gilbert .... Western
.... Allen Gilbert .... Western	
1983 .... Dick Reid .... Eastern	
.... George Ashby .... Central	In September 1988, the BFUSA and ABA
.... Allen Gilbert .... Western	merged to form the USBA.

USBA NATIONALS

1989 .... Carlos Hallon
1990 .... Sang Lee

MEN'S POCKET BILLIARD CHAMPIONS 1878-1983
Compiled by Charles Ursitti and Mike Shamos

The game of pocket billiards in the United States evolved slowly beginning in the 1830's. The present competitive form, known as straight pool or 14.1 continuous was not invented until 1910 and did not become the official championship game until 1912, when the term "pocket billiards" was first introduced. The earliest championship game was called "61-pool," a single-rack game with 15 numbered object balls. Each ball was worth a number of points equal to its numerical value; the first player to score at least 61 points was the winner. A match consisted of a race to a certain number of games, usually 21. This was the game played for the championship from 1878 until 1888.

Because a ball in 61-pool can be worth from 1 to 15 points, it was possible to win a match by sinking far fewer balls than one's opponent. This unfairness was corrected in 1889, when the game of "continuous pool" was introduced. The players still played individual fifteen-ball racks without a break ball, but each ball counted for only one point and the first player to reach a predetermined point total, usually 100, was the winner. The player who sank the last ball of a rack would break the full pack on the next rack. No ball had to be called on the break, so it was possible for long runs to occur extending over many racks. The record run at continuous pool is still 96, achieved by Alfredo De Oro in a non-championship game in 1911.

The break shot in continuous pool was very risky, since it is difficult to sink a ball in a controlled fashion when hitting a full rack of fifteen balls. Top players tended to play safety at the end of a rack rather than miss with the balls spread. This caused title games to become boring, as the audience could look forward to an exchange of safeties every fifteen balls. To eliminate the problem, Jerome Keogh, the champion in 1910 and teacher of future champion Irving Crane, suggested that the last ball of each rack be left free to be used as a target on the next rack. He proposed the name, "14 racked, 1 ball free," which became 14.1 continuous. It was adopted as the championship form for the tournament of April, 1912, won by Edward Ralph, who thus became the first straight pool champion.

At first, championships were established by donors, such as the Brunswick-Balke-Collender Corporation. These expired after a certain time and a new tournament had to be held to determine the next champion. In between tournaments, the champion was obliged to defend the title against challengers, who would meet the champion in a two-man match. Until the 1940's , this was the dominant method by which the title was decided, much as in boxing. It is therefore incorrect in most cases to associate a single champion with a particular year. Not all tournaments advertised as for the "title" are listed, but only those that were sanctioned by an appropriate governing body.

The table below lists all 206 times that the pocket billiard title has changed hands or become vacant. The date listed is the month in which the title change occurred. (In some cases, tournaments or matches took place over a period of many months lasting as long as a baseball season.) The "Champion" is the name of the titleholder. "Runner-Up" indicates the player who lost the title match, or, in the case of a tournament, the player finishing in second place. From 1878 through 1888, the game was 61-pool. Continuous pool was the championship game from 1889 to 1911 Straight pool has been the championship game since 1912.

Apr, 1878–Cyrille Dion .... Runner-Up–Samuel F. Knight
Aug, 1878–Gotthard Walhstrom .... Runner-Up–Cyrille Dion
Apr, 1879–Samuel F. Knight .... Runner-Up–Gotthard Walhstrom
Aug, 1879–Alonzo Morris .... Runner-Up–Samuel F. Knight
Oct, 1879–Gotthard Walhstrom .... Runner-Up–Alonzo Morris
Feb, 1880–Samuel F. Knight .... Runner-Up–Gotthard Walhstrom
May 1880–Gotthard Walhstrom .... Runner-Up–Samuel F. Knight
Jan, 1881–Gotthard Walhstrom .... Runner-Up–Albert M. Frey
Jun, 1881–Gotthard Walhstrom .... Runner-Up–Albert M. Frey
Jan, 1884–James L. Malone .... Runner-Up–Albert M. Frey, Joseph T. King (tie)
Mar, 1886–Albert M. Frey .... Runner-Up–James L. Malone
May, 1886–Albert M. Frey .... Runner-Up–James L. Malone
Feb, 1887–Albert M. Frey .... Runner-Up–James L. Malone
Apr, 1887–Albert M. Frey .... Runner-Up–James L. Malone
May, 1887–James L. Malone .... Runner-Up–Albert M. Frey
May, 1887–Alfredo De Oro .... Runner-Up–James L. Malone
Feb, 1888–Alfredo De Oro .... Runner-Up–James L. Malone
Feb, 1889–Albert M. Frey .... Runner-Up–Alfredo De Oro
Apr, 1889–Title vacant (Frey died)
Jun, 1889–Alfredo De Oro .... Runner-Up –Charles H. Manning
Apr, 1890–Alfredo De Oro .... Runner-Up–Charles H. Manning
May, 1890–Albert G. Powers .... Runner-Up–Alfredo De Oro
Jun, 1890–Charles H. Manning .... Runner-Up–Albert G. Powers
Aug, 1890–Charles H. Manning .... Runner-Up–George N. Kuntzsch
Oct, 1890–Charles H. Manning .... Runner-Up–Albert G. Powers
Jan, 1891–Albert G. Powers .... Runner-Up–Charles H. Manning
Mar, 1891–Albert G. Powers .... Runner-Up–William Clearwater
Mar, 1891–Albert G. Powers .... Runner-Up–P. H. Walsh
May, 1891–Alfredo De Oro .... Runner-Up–Albert G. Powers
Mar, 1893–Alfredo De Oro .... Runner-Up–Frank Sherman
Jun, 1893–Alfredo De Oro .... Runner-Up–P. H. Walsh
Dec, 1895–William Clearwater .... Runner-Up–Alfredo De Oro
Mar, 1896–William Clearwater .... Runner-Up–Jerome Keogh
Apr, 1896–William Clearwater .... Runner-Up–Alfredo De Oro
May, 1896–Alfredo De Oro .... Runner-Up–William Clearwater
Jun, 1896–Alfredo De Oro .... Runner-Up–Grant Eby
Fall, 1896–Herman E. Stewart .... Runner-Up–Alfredo De Oro
May, 1897–Grant Eby .... Runner-Up–Herman E. Stewart
Jun, 1897–Jerome Keogh .... Runner-Up–Grant Eby
Aug, 1897–Jerome Keogh .... Runner-Up–William Clearwater
Mar, 1898–William Clearwater .... Runner-Up–Jerome Keogh
Apr, 1898–Jerome Keogh .... Runner-Up–William Clearwater
Dec, 1898–Alfredo De Oro .... Runner-Up–Grant Eby, Frank Horgan (tie)
Jan, 1899–Alfredo De Oro ....
Apr, 1899–Alfredo De Oro .... Runner-Up–Jerome Keogh
Dec, 1899–Alfredo De Oro .... Runner-Up–Fred Payton
Apr, 1900–Alfredo De Oro .... Runner-Up–Jerome Keogh
Mar, 1901–Frank Sherman .... Runner-Up–Alfredo De Oro
Apr, 1901–Alfredo De Oro .... Runner-Up–Frank Sherman
Mar, 1902–William Clearwater .... Runner-Up–Charles Weston
May, 1902–Grant Eby .... Runner-Up–William Clearwater
Dec, 1902–Grant Eby .... Runner-Up–P. H. Walsh
May, 1903–Title vacant
Nov, 1904–Alfredo De Oro .... Runner-Up–Jerome Keogh
Nov, 1904–Alfredo De Oro .... Runner-Up–Jerome Keogh
Jan, 1905–Alfredo De Oro .... Runner-Up–Grant Eby
Mar, 1905–Jerome Keogh .... Runner Up–Alfredo De Oro
May, 1905–Alfredo De Oro .... Runner-Up–Jerome Keogh
Oct, 1905–Alfredo De Oro .... Runner-Up–William Clearwater
Dec, 1905–Thomas Hueston .... Runner-Up–Alfredo De Oro
Feb, 1906–Thomas Hueston .... Runner-Up–Charles Weston
Apr, 1906–Thomas Hueston .... Runner-Up–Joe W. Carney
May, 1906–John Horgan .... Runner-Up–Thomas Hueston

Oct, 1906–John Horgan .... Runner-Up–Horace B. ("Jess") Lean
Oct, 1906–Jerome Keogh .... Runner-Up–John Horgan
Nov, 1906–Jerome Keogh .... Runner-Up–Fred Tallman
Dec, 1906–Thomas Hueston .... Runner-Up–Jerome Keogh
Feb, 1907–Thomas Hueston .... Runner-Up–Edward Dawson
Apr, 1907–Thomas Hueston .... Runner-Up–Jerome Keogh
Apr, 1907–Thmas Hueston .... Runner-Up–William Clearwater
Jan, 1908–Thomas Hueston .... Runner-Up–Jerome Keogh
Jan, 1908–Title vacant
Apr, 1908–Frank Sherman .... Runner-Üp–Charles Weston
May, 1908–Alfredo De Oro .... Runner-Up–Frank Sherman
Oct, 1908–Alfredo De Oro .... Runner-Up–Bennie Allen
Nov, 1908–Thomas Hueston .... Runner-Up–Alfredo De Oro
Mar, 1909–Charles Weston .... Runner-Up–Thomas Hueston
May, 1909–Charles Weston .... Runner-Up–Horace B. ("Jess") Lean
Oct, 1909–John G. Kling .... Runner-Up–Charles Weston
Nov, 1909–Thomas Hueston .... Runner-Up–John G. Kling
Dec, 1909–Thomas Hueston .... Runner-Up–Bennie Allen
Feb, 1910–Jerome Keogh .... Runner-Up–Thomas Hueston
Mar, 1910–Jerome Keogh .... Runner-Up–Charles Weston
Apr, 1910–Jerome Keogh ...... ,.................................... Runner-Up–Thomas Safford
Sep, 1910–Jerome Keogh .... Runner-Up–Thomas Hueston
Oct, 1910–Jerome Keogh .... Runner-Up–Bennie Allen
Nov, 1910–Alfredo De Oro.................................... ,............... Runner-Up–Jerome Keogh
Jan, 1911–Alfredo De Oro .... Runner-Up–William Clearwater
Mar, 1911–Alfredo De Oro .... Runner·Up–Thomas Hueston
Apr, 1911–Alfredo De Oro .... Runner-Up–Jerome Keogh
May, 1911–Alfredo De Oro .... Runner-Up–Charles Weston
Nov, 1911–Title vacant
Apr, 1912–Edward Ralph .... Runner-Up–James Maturo
Jun, 1912–Alfredo De Oro .... Runner-Up–Edward Ralph
Nov, 1912–Alfredo De Oro .... Runner-Up–Frank Sherman
Jan, 1913–Alfredo De Oro .... Runner-Up–James Maturo
Feb, 1913–Alfredo De Oro .... Runner-Up–Thomas Hueston
Oct, 1913–Bennie Allen .... Runner-Up–Alfredo De Oro
Dec, 1913–Bennie Allen .... Runner-Up–Charles Weston
Jan, 1914–Bennie Allen .... Runner-Up–James Maturo
Apr, 1914–Bennie Allen .... Runner-Up–Edward Ralph
Jun, 1914–Bennie Allen .... Runner-Up–Ray R. Pratt
Dec, 1914–Bennie Allen .... Runner-Up–James Maturo
Dec, 1914–Title vacant
Mar, 1916–W. Emmett Blankenship .... Runner-Up–Johnny Layton
May, 1916–Johnny Layton .... Runner-Up–W. Emmett Blankenship
Sep, 1916–Frank Taberski .... Runner-Up–Johnny Layton
Oct, 1916–Frank Taberski .... Runner-Up–Ralph Greenleaf
Nov, 1916–Frank Taberski .... Runner-Up–Edward Ralph
Jan, 1917–Frank Taberski .... Runner-Up–James Maturo
Feb, 1917–Frank Taberski .... Runner-Up–Louis Kreuter
Apr, 1917–Frank Taberski .... Runner-Up–Bennie Allen
May, 1917–Frank Taberski .... Runner-Up–Larry Stoutenberg
Oct, 1917–Frank Taberski .... Runner-Up–Joe Concannon
Nov, 1917–Frank Taberski .... Runner-Up–Louis Kreuter
Jan, 1918–Frank Taberski .... Runner-Up–Ralph Greenleaf
Jan, 1918–Title vacant
Dec, 1919–Ralph Greenleaf .... Runner-Up–Bennie Allen
Nov, 1920–Ralph Greenleaf .... Runner-Up–Arthur Woods
Oct, 1921–Ralph Greenleaf .... Runner-Up–Arthur Woods
Dec, 1921–Ralph Greenleaf .... Runner-Up–Arthur Woods
Feb, 1922–Ralph Greenleaf .... Runner-Up–Thomas Hueston
May, 1922–Ralph Greenleaf .... Runner-Up–Walter Franklin
Oct, 1922–Ralph Greenleaf .... Runner-Up–Bennie Allen
Dec, 1922–Ralph Greenleaf .... Runner-Up–Arthur Church
Jan, 1923–Ralph Greenleaf .... Runner-Up–Thomas Hueston

Apr, 1924–Ralph Greenleaf .... Runner-Up–Bennie Allen
Apr, 1925–Frank Taberski .... Runner-Up–Ralph Greenleaf
Apr, 1926–Title vacant
Nov, 1926–Ralph Greenleaf .... Runner-Up–Erwin Rudolph
Jan, 1927–Erwin Rudolph .... Runner-Up–Ralph Greenleaf
Mar, 1927–Erwin Rudolph .... Runner-Up–Harry Oswald
May, 1927–Thomas Hueston .... Runner-Up–Erwin Rudolph
Sep, 1927–Frank Taberski .... Runner-Up–Thomas Hueston
Nov, 1927–Frank Taberski .... Runner-Up–Pasquale Natalie
Jan, 1928–Frank Taberski .... Runner-Up–Arthur Woods
Mar, 1928–Ralph Greenleaf .... Runner-Up–Frank Taberski
May, 1928–Ralph Greenleaf .... Runner-Up–Andrew St. Jean
Dec, 1928–Frank Taberski .... Runner-Up–Ralph Greenleaf
Dec, 1929–Ralph Greenleaf .... Runner-Up–Erwin Rudolph
Dec, 1930–Erwin Rudolph .... Runner-Up–Ralph Greenleaf
Dec, 1931–Ralph Greenleaf .... Runner-Up–George Kelly
Dec, 1932–Ralph Greenleaf .... Runner-Up–Jimmy Caras
May, 1933–Ralph Greenleaf .... Runner-Up–Andrew Ponzi
Dec, 1933–Erwin Rudolph .... Runner-Up–Andrew Ponzi
Feb, 1934–Andrew Ponzi .... Runner-Up–Erwin Rudolph
1934–Title vacant
Dec, 1935–Jimmy Caras .... Runner-Up–Erwin Rudolph
Apr, 1936–Jimmy Caras .... Runner-Up–Erwin Rudolph
Apr, 1937–Ralph Greenleaf .... Runner-Up–Andrew Ponzi
Dec, 1937–Ralph Greenleaf .... Runner-Up–Irving Crane
Mar, 1938–Jimmy Caras .... Runner-Up–Andrew Ponzi
Apr, 1938–Jimmy Caras .... Runner-Up–Andrew Ponzi
Apr, 1940–Andrew Ponzi .... Runner-Up–Jimmy Caras
May, 1941–Willie Mosconi .... Runner-Up–Andrew Ponzi
Nov, 1941–Erwin Rudolph .... Runner-Up–Irving Crane
May, 1942–Irving Crane .... Runner-Up–Erwin Rudolph
Dec, 1942–Willie Mosconi .... Runner-Up–Andrew Ponzi
Apr, 1943–Andrew Ponzi .... Runner-Up–Willie Mosconi
Dec, 1943–Andrew Ponzi .... Runner-Up–Irving Crane
Mar, 1944–Willie Mosconi .... Runner-Up–Andrew Ponzi
Feb, 1945–Willie Mosconi .... Runner-Up–Ralph Greenleaf
Mar, 1946–Willie Mosconi .... Runner-Up–Jimmy Caras
Dec, 1946–Willie Mosconi .... Runner-Up–Irving Crane
Dec, 1946–Irving Crane .... Runner-Up–Willie Mosconi
May, 1947–Willie Mosconi .... Runner-Up–Irving Crane
Nov, 1947–Willie Mosconi .... Runner-Up–Jimmy Caras
Mar, 1948–Willie Mosconi .... Runner-Up–Andrew Ponzi
Feb, 1949–Jimmy Caras .... Runner-Up–Willie Mosconi
Feb, 1950–Willie Mosconi .... Runner-Up–Irving Crane
Jan, 1951–Willie Mosconi .... Runner-Up–Irving Crane
Feb, 1951–Willie Mosconi .... Runner-Up–Irving Crane
Apr, 1952–Willie Mosconi .... Runner-Up–Irving Crane
Mar, 1953–Willie Mosconi .... Runner-Up–Joe Procita
Mar, 1955–Willie Mosconi .... Runner-Up–Joe Procita
Apr, 1955–Irving Crane .... Runner-Up–Willie Mosconi
Dec, 1955–Willie Mosconi .... Runner-Up–Irving Crane
Feb, 1956–Willie Mosconi .... Runner-Up–Jimmy Caras
Mar, 1956–Willie Mosconi .... Runner-Up–Jimmy Moore
Apr, 1956–Willie Mosconi .... Runner-Up–Irving Crane
Apr, 1963–Luther Lassiter .... Runner-Up–Jimmy Moore
Aug, 1963–Luther Lassiter .... Runner-Up–Jimmy Moore
Mar, 1964–Luther Lassiter .... Runner-Up–Arthur Cranfield
Sep, 1964–Arthur Cranfield .... Runner-Up–Luther Lassiter
Mar, 1965–Joe Balsis .... Runner-Up–Jimmy Moore
Mar, 1966–Luther Lassiter .... Runner-Up–Cisero Murphy
Dec, 1966–Luther Lassiter .... Runner-Up–Cisero Murphy

Apr, 1967–Luther Lassiter .... Runner-Up–Jack Breit
Dec, 1967–Luther Lassiter .... Runner-Up–Jack Breit
Apr, 1968–Irving Crane .... Runner-Up–Luther Lassiter
Feb, 1969–Ed Kelly .... Runner-Up–Cisero Murphy
Feb, 1970–Irving Crane .... Runner-Up–Steve Mizerak
Feb, 1971–Ray Martin .... Runner-Up–Joe Balsis
Feb, 1972–Irving Crane .... Runner-Up–Lou Butera
Feb, 1973–Lou Butera .... Runner-Up–Irving Crane
Feb, 1974–Ray Martin .... Runner-Up–Allen Hopkins
Aug, 1976–Larry Lisciotti .... Runner-Up–Steve Mizerak
Aug, 1977–Allen Hopkins .... Runner-Up–Pete Margo
Aug, 1978–Ray Martin .... Runner-Up–Allen Hopkins
Aug, 1979–Mike Sigel .... Runner-Up–Joe Balsis
Aug, 1980–Nick Varner .... Runner-Up–Mike Sigel
Aug, 1981–Mike Sigel .... Runner-Up–Nick Varner
Aug, 1982–Steve Mizerak .... Runner-Up–Danny DiLiberto
Aug, 1983–Steve Mizerak .... Runner-Up–Jimmy Fusco

WORLD THREE CUSHION CHAMPIONS (Professional)

1878	Leon Magnus		1919	Robert L. Cannefax
1899	W. H. Catton		1920	John Layton
1900	Eugene Carter		1921	Augie Kieckhefer
1900	Lloyd Jevne		1921-22	John Layton
1907	Harry P. Cline		1923	Tiff Denton
1908	John W. Daly		1924-25	Robert L. Cannefax
1908	Thomas Hueston		1926	Otto Reiselt
1908	Alfredo De Oro		1927	Augie Kieckhefer
1909	Alfredo De Oro		1927	Otto Reiselt
1910	Fred Eames		1928-30	John Layton
1910	Thomas Hueston		1931	Arthur Thurnblad
1910	Alfredo De Oro		1932	Augie Kieckhefer
1910	John W. Daly		1933	Welker Cochran
1911	Alfredo De Oro		1934	John Layton
1912	Joseph W. Carney		1935	Welker Cochran
1912	John Horgan		1936	William Hoppe
1913-14	Alfredo De Oro		1936-37	Welker Cochran
1915	George Moore		1938	Roger Conti
1915	William H. Huey		1939	Joseph Chamaco
1915	Alfredo De Oro		1940-43	William F. Hoppe
1916	Charles Ellis		1944-46	Welker Cochran
1916	Charles McCourt		1947-52	William F. Hoppe
1916	Hugh Heal		1953	Raymond Kilgore
1916	George Moore		1954	Harold Worst
1917	Charles McCourt		1964	Arthur Rubin
1917	Robert L. Cannefax		1969	Juan Navarra
1917	Alfredo De Oro		1972	Juan Navarra
1918	Augie Kieckhefer		1984	Ludo Dielis
1919	Alfredo De Oro			

Three Cushion Records

High Run–Game (50 points) .... Willie Hoppe 20 1928
High Run–Match (360 & 1,000 points) .... Willie Hoppe 15 1936-50
High Average–Game (50 points) .... Otto Reiselt 3.13 1926
High Grand Average–Match (1,400 points) .... Willie Hoppe 1.18 1947
High Grand Average–Tournament .... Willie Hoppe 1.33 1950

WORLD THREE CUSHION CHAMPIONS (Amateur)

1928-29 .... Edmond Soussa, Egypt	1960 .... Rene Vingerhoedt, Belgium
1930 .... H. J. Robyns, Holland	1961 .... Adolfo Suarez, Peru
1931 .... Enrique Miro, Spain	1963-73 .... Raymond Ceulemans, Belgium
1932-33 .... H. J. Robyns, Holland	1974 .... Nobuaki Kobayashi, Japan
1934 .... Claudio Puigvert, Spain	1975-80 .... Raymond Ceulemans, Belgium
1935 .... Alfredo Lagache, France	1981 .... Ludo Dielis, Belgium
1936 .... Edward L. Lee, U.S.A.	1982 .... Rini Van Bracht, Holland
1937 .... Alfredo Lagache, France	1983 .... Raymond Ceulemans, Belgium
1938 .... Augusto Vergez, Argentina	1984 .... Nabuaki Kobayashi, Japan
1948 .... Rene Vingerhoedt, Belgium	1985 .... Raymond Ceulemans, Belgium
1952 .... Pedro L. Carrera, Argentina	1986 .... Avelino Rico, Spain
1953 & 58 .... Enrique Navarra, Argentina	1987 .... Torbjorn Blomdahl, Sweden

Three Cushion Records

High Run (U.S.A.)–Game (50 points) .... Bill Hawkins 19 1977
High Run–Game (60 points) .... Marcello Lopez 15 1964
.... R. Ceulemans 15 1975
.... A. Gonzales 15 1979
High Average–Game (60 points) .... R. Ceulemans 2.5 1966
High Grand Average–Tournament .... R. Ceulemans 1.679 1978

BCA SANCTIONING OF BILLIARD TOURNAMENTS

BCA offers tournament sanctioning for amateur and professional tournaments for a nominal fee. This official sanction signifies the tournament's authenticity. With each sanction, the sponsor shall receive the following:

- Official Rules & Record Book
- Double Elimination pairing charts
- Official Tournament Report Forms
- Official Tournament Sanction Certificate
- Advance listing in the BCA BREAK newsletter
- Recognition of the tournament and winner in the next BCA Official Rules and Record Book

- -

Please send us a Sanction Application for:

(type of tournament) _____

Name _____

Company _____

Address_____

City _____ State _____ Zip _____

Home Phone _____ Business Phone _____

Return to: BCA, 1901 Broadway St., Suite 310, Iowa City, IA 52240

Together,
We can make billiards the sport of the '90s.

By becoming a member of BCA, you will become part of the industry-wide movement to promote pool and billiards.

Manufacturer, Distributor, Importer Member $1000
    (Represented by 12 members on the board)
Associate Member (has $1/2$ vote) 500
Retail Member 250
Proprietor Member
    8 + tables 100
    1-7 tables 50
Coin Machine Operator 100

☐ *YES, I would like to become a member of BCA.*

Name _____

Company Name _____

Address _____

City _____ State _____ Zip _____

Date _____ Phone _____

Signature _____

☐ My check for $ _____ is enclosed.

Return to: BCA, 1901 Broadway St., Suite 310, Iowa City, IA 52240

NOTES